# Beyond the Facade

## Unveiling the Truth About Toxic Families

By
Well-Being Publishing

To You,

*Thank you!*

# Contents

# The Invisible Wounds of Toxic Upbringing

At the very core of our being, the family is supposed to be our sanctuary, a safe haven where love and support are unconditional. Unfortunately, for many, the reality is starkly different. The upbringing that was meant to nurture instead inflicts invisible wounds, deep and lasting. These are wounds that don't bleed externally but hemorrhage internally, affecting the essence of who we are and who we can become. This book is dedicated to unveiling those wounds, understanding their origins, and paving a path forward for healing and empowerment.

The term 'toxic upbringing' might seem harsh to some, but it precisely encapsulates the environment that countless individuals have grown up in. Such environments are characterized not by the overt signs of unhealthy dynamics but by the subtleties of emotional neglect, manipulation, and a consistent lack of empathy. The damage inflicted by these behaviors is not immediately visible, and thus, it's all too easy for it to be dismissed or overlooked, even by those who bear its scars.

Moving through life with these invisible wounds often means navigating a world that seems not to understand or, at times, not to care. It means struggling with self-doubt, with feelings of unworthiness, and with the daunting task of building healthy relationships when your blueprint was anything but healthy. This book argues that while the wounds may be invisible and the struggles internal, the path toward healing is tangible and attainable.

One of the central goals here is to validate your experiences. If you've ever felt alone in your pain, misunderstood by friends, or dismissed by family members, know that your feelings and experiences are real and deserving of acknowledgment. The validation of one's pain is a critical step on the journey of healing.

We will provide insights into the dynamics of toxic family environments, helping you to recognize patterns that may have seemed normal but were anything but. Through understanding, there's an opportunity to see your experiences from a new perspective, one that fosters compassion for yourself and allows for a reevaluation of what you've been through.

Support is another pillar of our mission. Healing from a toxic upbringing is not a journey that should be undertaken alone. This book aims to be a companion in your healing process, offering guidance, encouragement, and strategies to not only overcome but to thrive beyond the shadows of your upbringing.

Raising awareness is crucial. By shedding light on the subtleties of toxic family dynamics, we can begin to shift societal understanding and empathy towards those who have experienced this form of upbringing. It's about changing the narrative from one of isolation and shame to one of awareness, support, and ultimately transformation.

Empowerment is the destination. Moving beyond the past isn't just about healing; it's about reclaiming the narrative of your life, discovering your inherent worth, and reshaping your future with intention and purpose. It's about recognizing that the toxic behaviors of others reflect their limitations, not your value.

The journey of healing and empowerment is not linear, nor is it prescriptive. It's uniquely personal, with ebbs and flows, triumphs, and setbacks. This book acknowledges the complexity of this journey and offers a variety of tools and strategies, recognizing that what works for one may not work for another.

Whether you're an adult child of toxic parents, a therapist seeking to support clients navigating these experiences, or simply someone looking to understand and help a loved one, this book is for you. It's a guide for healing, a source of understanding, and a beacon of hope for anyone who has ever felt the impact of a toxic upbringing.

Embarking on this journey might seem daunting, but it's also an act of profound courage. It's a declaration that the patterns of the past will not define the possibilities of the future. It's an assertion that you are worthy of love, respect, and a fulfilling life, regardless of the environment you were raised in.

As we move through the chapters of this book, keep an open heart and an open mind. Healing is not just about moving away from something; it's about moving towards something - a life of authenticity, peace, and burgeoning joy. The road might be rocky, but the destination is luminous with potential.

So, let's begin this journey together, with compassion, understanding, and a relentless belief in the possibility of transformation. The wounds may be invisible, but the healing will be palpable, not just in your life but in the lives of those around you. Together, we can turn the tide of toxicity, one healing moment at a time.

Remember, your past doesn't have to dictate your future. The power to redefine your life and cultivate happiness lies within you. Let this book be a tool in your arsenal, a friend on your path, and a reminder of the strength and resilience that dwells within your spirit. The journey ahead is not just about overcoming; it's about thriving, growing, and discovering the boundless potential of a life unshackled by the past.

# Chapter 1:
# Understanding Toxic Family Dynamics

To embark on a journey of healing and empowerment, it's essential to first understand the landscape we're navigating. Toxic family dynamics can creep in silently, often masqueraded as normalcy until we find our spirits wearied, our relationships strained, and our sense of self-diluted. This chapter lays the foundational work, dissecting what makes a family dynamic toxic, pinpointing common characteristics, and delving into the profound impact such environments have on individual family members. At its core, toxicity in families manifests through patterns of behavior that undermine the emotional and psychological well-being of its members. These patterns can range from subtle manipulations to overt abuse, leaving scars that might not be visible but are deeply felt. Understanding these dynamics is not about assigning blame but about recognizing the influences that have shaped our interactions and internal dialogue. It's a step towards freeing ourselves from cycles of dysfunction, towards finding our voices, and reclaiming our right to healthy, fulfilling relationships. By illuminating the dark corners of toxic family dynamics, we not only validate our experiences but also pave the path towards healing and empowerment. With each insight gained, we edge closer to breaking free from the chains of our upbringing, equipped with the knowledge and strength to foster healthier connections with ourselves and others.

## Defining Toxicity in the Family Context

In our journey to understand toxic family dynamics, it's essential to delve into what we mean by 'toxicity' within the family context. The term 'toxic' can be broad and subjective, yet at its core, it points to behaviors and environments that are detrimental to one's psychological and emotional well-being. In family settings, toxicity manifests through patterns of abuse, neglect, manipulation, and control that erode the individual's sense of self, autonomy, and capacity for healthy relationships.

Toxicity in families isn't always overt; it can be subtle, masked by expressions of care or concern, or woven into the fabric of day-to-day interactions that, on the surface, seem benign. It's the accumulation of these interactions over time that creates an atmosphere where individuals feel diminished, trapped, or stifled, leading to long-term emotional and psychological harm.

At its heart, family toxicity violates the basic expectation of family as a source of support, love, and safety. Families are supposed to be the foundational unit that nurtures and prepares us for the external world. When these relationships become sources of hurt and betrayal, the effects can be deeply disorienting and wounding.

Understanding the nuances of toxic behavior in families requires recognizing the diverse forms it can take. It includes, but is not limited to, physical abuse, emotional manipulation, neglect, gaslighting, and financial exploitation. Each of these behaviors, in isolation or combination, can undermine a person's foundation of safety and self-worth.

One of the profound challenges in defining family toxicity is the societal reluctance to acknowledge harmful behavior within the sanctity of the family unit. This societal hesitation often silences the victims, shrouding family dynamics in secrecy and shame. It's a perplexing paradox; the very institution revered for its role in personal and social stability can also be a crucible for profound suffering.

Victims of toxic family environments frequently struggle with internalized guilt and shame. The familial tie adds complexity to their pain, engendering a conflict between the innate desire for familial connection and the instinct for self-preservation. Recognizing and acknowledging this inner turmoil is a vital step in healing from toxic family experiences.

Defining toxicity in family contexts also involves understanding the spectrum of intensity. Not all negative behaviors constitute toxicity. It's the persistent, detrimental patterns that erode one's sense of self and emotional health that are deeply concerning. This distinction is crucial for both recognizing toxic situations and initiating steps toward healing and recovery.

A critical aspect of toxicity is its intergenerational nature. Often, toxic behaviors and patterns are passed down, unconsciously perpetuated by those who were themselves victims. Recognizing this cycle is pivotal not only for healing but also for breaking the chain of toxicity, preventing its transmission to future generations.

It's also essential to underscore that toxicity does not define a person's entirety. Individuals who exhibit toxic behaviors are often acting out of their unresolved pains and traumas. This understanding does not excuse the behavior but underscores the complexity of human relationships and the potential for change.

Addressing and healing from family toxicity is a journey that requires courage, introspection, and support. It often involves setting boundaries, seeking therapy, and rebuilding a sense of self outside the family narrative. It's a process of reclaiming one's autonomy, worth, and capacity for healthy relationships.

Empowerment is a crucial theme in navigating family toxicity. Recognizing one's worth, rights, and needs lays the groundwork for transformative change. Although the journey may be fraught with challenges and setbacks, it is also filled with potential for growth, resilience, and healing.

Moreover, healing from toxic family dynamics is not a solitary journey. Creating a supportive network—whether through friends, therapy, support groups, or online communities—can provide the validation, understanding, and encouragement needed to navigate this intricate path.

Fostering open, honest conversations about family toxicity is vital for raising awareness and supporting others in similar situations. It's through shared stories and experiences that the veil of secrecy and shame can be lifted, illuminating pathways to healing and empowerment.

Lastly, embracing one's story, with all its pain and resilience, is a powerful act of self-affirmation. It's a declaration that, despite the past, one can forge a future grounded in self-respect, healthy relationships, and well-being. The journey from toxicity to empowerment is a testament to the human spirit's capacity for renewal and transformation.

In defining toxicity within the family context, we uncover not only the layers of harm and pain but also the potential for healing and growth. It's a narrative of moving beyond the shadows, embracing one's worth, and crafting a life characterized by healthy relationships and inner peace. This journey, while challenging, is rich with opportunity for transformation, resilience, and profound self-discovery.

## Common Characteristics of Toxic Families

In exploring the landscape of toxic family dynamics, it becomes crystal clear that certain patterns and behaviors recurrently emerge amidst the chaos. These characteristics, though varied and complex, construct a framework through which we can begin to understand the profound impact of toxicity within familial relationships. This understanding is pivotal, not just for those who have lived through these experiences but also for those who seek to support them on their journey toward healing.

Toxic families often operate under a thick veil of denial, a common trait that serves to protect the family image while simultaneously invalidating the experiences and feelings of its members. This denial isn't merely about ignoring problems but encompasses an active dismissal of any narratives that challenge the family's prescribed version of reality. It's a silencing mechanism, one that leaves individuals feeling isolated and questioning their own perceptions.

Another hallmark of toxic families is the presence of rigid roles assigned to each family member. These roles, whether it be the caretaker, the scapegoat, or the golden child, trap individuals in a narrow identity, limiting their freedom to express the full breadth of their personality and emotions. Such roles can define and restrict individuals long into adulthood, influencing their relationship choices and self-esteem.

Communication within toxic families is characteristically poor, often infused with criticism, sarcasm, and contempt rather than clarity, empathy, and respect. Conversations that should foster connection and understanding become battlegrounds, with certain members dominating the dialogue while others recede into silence, fearful of repercussions should they speak their truth.

Control is a central element in these family systems. It can manifest overtly through overt demands and restrictions or covertly through guilt and emotional manipulation. Family members may find their autonomy stifled, with significant decisions about their lives, from career choices to personal relationships, being unduly influenced or outright controlled by others in the family.

Boundaries are frequently absent or disrespected in toxic families. What should be healthy limits that protect individual well-being and foster mutual respect are often blurred or violated. This lack of boundaries can lead to enmeshment, where individual identities are subsumed into the family fabric, leaving little room for personal growth or independence.

Conflicts are inevitable in any relationship, yet in toxic families, the way conflicts are handled can be particularly destructive. Rather than seeking resolution and understanding, conflicts are often characterized by blame, avoidance, or escalation into intense verbal or even physical altercations. The inability to resolve conflicts healthily perpetuates cycles of resentment and hurt.

In toxic families, love and affection may be conditional, used as tools for manipulation and control. Members may find themselves in a constant battle to earn love through compliance and performance, leading to a profound sense of unworthiness and insecurity in their relationships.

The fallout from growing up in a toxic family environment is not just emotional but can have significant psychological impacts. Anxiety, depression, low self-esteem, and difficulties forming healthy relationships are common among those who've navigated this challenging upbringing. Recognizing these effects is a crucial step towards healing.

In the midst of these characteristics, it's vital to understand the resilience and strength that can emerge. Many find within themselves an incredible capacity for empathy, deep introspective insight, and the ability to foster meaningful relationships outside of their family of origin. The journey of healing and recovery can unveil these qualities, offering a path to a more fulfilling and authentic life.

It's also important to acknowledge that breaking free from toxic family patterns is not an act of betrayal or selfishness. It's a courageous step toward self-preservation and health. Establishing boundaries, seeking supportive networks, and embracing one's own truths are necessary measures on the path to recovery.

Understanding the common characteristics of toxic families paves the way for recognition and acknowledgment of one's experiences. It's about removing the mantles of shame and guilt that many carry and replacing them with validation and self-compassion. This recognition is the first step on the journey towards healing and empowerment.

Change is not only possible but is within reach. While the scars of the past might shape part of who we are, they don't have to define us. Unlearning harmful patterns, reconnecting with our authentic selves, and building new, healthy relationships are all part of the transformative process that lies ahead.

At the heart of moving beyond toxicity is the belief in one's worth and the unshakeable right to a life of respect, love, and happiness. The path forward might not be easy, but it's paved with opportunities for growth, healing, and the discovery of a strength that perhaps, until now, was unrecognizable.

Finally, it's essential to remember that you're not alone on this journey. There's a community of survivors, each with their own story, who understand the complex emotions and challenges you face. Together, there's hope for healing, for breaking the cycles of toxicity, and for building a future that honors your experiences, resilience, and capacity for love.

## The Impact on Individual Family Members

Within the complex web of toxic family dynamics, the ripple effects felt by each individual member are profound and far-reaching. Understanding these impacts is crucial for anyone navigating the path of healing and self-discovery. It's about peeling back the layers to uncover how deeply rooted issues have influenced not only relationships within the family but also with oneself.

The first ripple often felt is the erosion of self-esteem. When a family's toxicity manifests through constant criticism, comparison, or dismissal, individuals start to see themselves through this distorted lens. They may struggle with feelings of inadequacy, questioning their worth and capabilities. This isn't just a phase; it can define how they approach relationships, challenges, and their own goals for much of their life.

Another significant impact is the development of trust issues. In environments where manipulation and unpredictability are commonplace, members learn to tense up, awaiting the next emotional upheaval. This heightened state of alert becomes a baseline, influencing how they interact with the world. Trust isn't easy to come by when you've learned to expect the rug to be pulled out from under you at any moment.

Communication skills, too, bear the brunt of toxic dynamics. Individuals may swing from extreme passivity to aggressive assertiveness, struggling to find that healthy middle ground. The models they've had for expressing needs, desires, or disagreements were skewed, leaving them to navigate the complex world of interpersonal interactions without a clear compass.

Mental health concerns, such as anxiety and depression, are also significantly more prevalent. The constant stress of navigating a toxic environment can leave individuals in a perpetual state of fight or flight, wearing down both mental and physical health over time. The shadow of these issues often stretches far into adulthood, even long after the family environment has been left behind.

The susceptibility to entering toxic relationships outside the family unit increases as well. Patterns learned in childhood become the templates for future relationships unless actively unlearned. It's not uncommon for survivors of toxic families to find themselves in similar dynamics at work, in friendships, or romantic relationships, perpetuating the cycle of toxicity they're familiar with.

Personal boundaries become a concept that many struggle with. Growing up in an environment where boundaries were either violated or non-existent leaves individuals unsure of how to set and maintain healthy limits. The journey to understanding and asserting one's own boundaries is often fraught with guilt, confusion, and setbacks.

One of the more insidious effects is the internalization of toxic behaviors. Without other models, individuals may unconsciously replicate the very actions and attitudes that hurt them. Recognizing and breaking this cycle is a monumental part of the healing process, yet it's one of the most challenging aspects to tackle.

Survivors may also grapple with loneliness and isolation. The intense loyalty demanded by toxic family systems often prevents the formation of external support networks. Even if physical distance is achieved, the emotional and psychological barriers can make reaching out for help or forming new connections incredibly daunting.

Identity confusion is another common impact. Individuals raised in toxic environments often have to suppress their own needs, desires, and personalities to navigate the volatility of their home life.

Unraveling who they are beyond those survival mechanisms is a journey of self-discovery that requires patience, compassion, and often, professional support.

For those who manage to break away from the toxic family environment, there's often a lingering sense of guilt and obligation. The familial tie, shaped by cultural, societal, and personal beliefs, weighs heavily, making the decision to distance oneself fraught with internal conflict. This guilt can sabotage efforts to heal and forge a healthier path forward.

Furthermore, the perception of the world and one's place within it can be deeply affected. A worldview shaped by toxic dynamics is one of skepticism, fear, and limitation. Expanding beyond that to see the world as a place of possibility and abundance requires not just a shift in perspective but a complete overhaul of deeply ingrained beliefs.

Resilience, ironically, can also emerge as a powerful outcome. Those who have navigated the treacherous waters of toxic family dynamics often develop a strength and adaptability that are unparalleled. Recognizing and harnessing this resilience is key to transforming past pain into a force for positive change in one's life.

Lastly, the journey towards healing and self-actualization is marked by an intense struggle between the desire for familial connection and the need for self-preservation. Finding a balance, or choosing one path over the other, is a deeply personal process that unfolds differently for everyone. It's a testament to the complexity of human relationships and the enduring quest for self-understanding and peace.

As we explore the impacts of toxic family dynamics on individual family members, it's essential to approach the topic with empathy, openness, and a belief in the possibility of healing and transformation. Each person's experience is unique, yet the themes are universal, echoing the shared human need for connection, respect, and love.

Understanding these impacts is not just an academic exercise; it's a crucial step on the path to healing and empowerment.

14

# Chapter 2:
# Emotional Immaturity and Unavailability

As we delve into the heart of emotional immaturity and unavailability, it's crucial to recognize that these traits are not mere character flaws but profound barriers to forming meaningful, healthy relationships. Emotional immaturity in parents can often go unnoticed, mistaken as eccentricity or a demanding nature, but its impact on family dynamics and the emotional well-being of children is far-reaching. This chapter seeks to unravel the complexities of emotional immaturity, shedding light on how such unavailability breeds a toxic environment that stiflops personal growth and fosters insecurity. From withdrawing affection to negating the child's feelings, emotionally immature parents unwittingly set the stage for a cycle of emotional neglect. Unmasking the profiles of emotionally immature parents is the first step toward understanding the gravity of their influence. By learning to identify these characteristics, we empower ourselves not just to heal but to break the perpetuating cycle of toxicity, embracing the possibility of forging nurturing connections, both with ourselves and with others. The path to healing and growth lies in acknowledging the deep-seated issues stemming from such unavailability, daring to confront the pain, and cultivating resilience. Together, let's embark on this journey towards healing, guiding our steps towards a future where emotional maturity and availability are not just ideals but realities within our relationships.

## Profiles of Emotionally Immature Parents

Understanding the different profiles of emotionally immature parents is essential for both recognizing the dynamics that played out in your upbringing and for nurturing your healing journey. Emotionally immature parents often fall into distinct categories, each with their own patterns of behavior that can impact children in profound ways.

Firstly, there's the *Emotional Outsourcer*. This type of parent looks to their child to fulfill their emotional needs, treating their child more like a partner or friend than their offspring. Such parents often share inappropriate information with their child, rely on them for emotional support, or expect them to manage the parent's moods and problems. This inversion of roles can leave children feeling burdened, overly responsible for others' feelings, and unsure about the boundaries of normal parent-child relationships.

Another profile is the *Authoritarian Disciplinarian*. This parent rules with an iron fist, valuing discipline over dialogue. They may have rigid standards and a my-way-or-the-highway attitude, often leading to a household environment where fear, rather than love, is the primary motivator. Children of such parents might become excellent rule-followers, but they often struggle with self-esteem, innovation, and understanding their worth outside of achievement and obedience.

The *Detached Protector* is a parent who, on the surface, seems to provide for all the child's needs—except emotional connection. They're often physically present but emotionally distant, showing little interest in their child's inner life. This lack of emotional availability can lead children to question their own value and to struggle with forming deep, meaningful relationships later in life.

On the flip side is the *Enmeshed Caregiver*. This parent blurs or entirely disregards the boundaries between themselves and their child, often treating the child as an extension of themselves. They may heavily depend on their child for companionship or see their child's achievements and failures as their own. This can lead to issues with autonomy and individuation in the child, making it difficult for them to carve out their own identity.

The *Critical Observer* is an emotionally immature parent who is overly focused on faults and mistakes. They may have unrealistically high expectations and be quick to point out where their child falls short, rarely providing the unconditional positive regard that fosters healthy self-esteem. Children of such parents might become perfectionists, constantly chasing approval that feels just out of reach.

A perhaps more subtle, yet enormously impactful, profile is the *Emotional Volcano.* These parents are unpredictable, with their emotional explosions and dramatic mood swings creating an environment of constant instability. Walking on eggshells becomes a way of life for their children, who often develop into adults that are hyper-vigilant to the moods and needs of others, sometimes at the cost of their own emotional well-being.

The *Silent Withholder* uses withdrawal as a means of control or punishment. Unlike the Detached Protector, this parent actively withholds affection, approval, or communication as a response to perceived slights or as a method of discipline. Children of these parents may grow up feeling love is conditional and must be earned by pleasing the withholder, often leading to codependent relationship patterns.

The *Fear-Driven Adviser* operates from a place of their own anxieties, projecting fears onto their children and discouraging risk-taking or independence. They often mean well, believing they're protecting their child, but their constant worry can smother initiative and foster a mindset that the world is a dangerous place best navigated with caution.

The *Fantasy Builder* parent lives in a world of 'what could be' instead of 'what is,' always chasing dreams without laying down the realistic groundwork necessary to achieve them. For their children, this can manifest in a life fraught with instability and disappointment, or a pressure to fulfill the dreams their parents couldn't.

Lastly, the *Comparative Competitor*. This parent sees everything as a competition, often comparing their child to siblings, peers, or even themselves at that age. This unending comparison can erode a child's sense of self-worth and contribute to a lifelong habit of measuring their value against that of others.

Recognizing these profiles in our parents is not about placing blame or remaining stuck in the past. It's about gaining clarity on the roots of our emotional experiences, validating our feelings, and understanding the significant influence our upbringing has had on our personalities and behaviors. This awareness serves as a springboard for healing, empowering us to break free from limiting patterns and to cultivate healthier, more fulfilling relationships moving forward.

Indeed, the journey to healing is multifaceted and deeply personal. Embracing the complexity of our parents' humanity while acknowledging the pain we've endured allows us to navigate the path toward recovery with grace and compassion. Remember, healing is not linear and requires patience, support, and self-compassion.

Moreover, as we understand the backdrop against which our early experiences unfolded, we can begin to release the hold these patterns may have on us. In identifying the traits of emotionally immature parents, we unearth tools to rebuild our sense of self, redefining our boundaries, and reimagining what love and healthy relationships look like for us.

In owning our stories and understanding the roles that our parents have played, we unlock the power to script new narratives that honor our resilience, our worth, and our capacity to love deeply - in ways that perhaps our parents couldn't. The knowledge of these profiles illuminates the path to emancipation from past hurts, guiding us toward a future where we are the architects of our own peace and happiness.

Let this exploration be a beacon of hope, reaffirming that although we cannot change the past, we possess the strength and agency to shape a vibrant, fulfilling, and empowered future. It's within this understanding and acceptance that we find the keys to unlocking our boundless potential, breaking the chains of emotional immaturity that have held us bound, and stepping into the light of our own, self-defined horizon.

## How Emotional Neglect Perpetuates Family Toxicity

Emotional neglect within the family unit is a silent propagator of toxicity, often skulking beneath overt behaviors and patterns that seem more palpable. Understanding how emotional neglect weaves its web within the family structure is imperative for those journeying towards healing and for those supporting them. It's a nuanced issue that, when left unaddressed, perpetuates a cycle of pain and misunderstanding that can span generations.

At its core, emotional neglect in a family context happens when the emotional needs of its members, especially children, are consistently ignored, minimized, or invalidated. This can be particularly destructive because it communicates a message of worthlessness and invisibility to the child. It's not about the occasional oversight; it's about a persistent pattern that deeply imbeds a sense of inadequacy and unimportance in the child's psyche.

Children growing up in such environments often struggle to identify their feelings or manage them constructively. The absence of emotional validation teaches them to disregard their own experiences, leading to difficulties in acknowledging or expressing emotions as adults. This internal emotional neglect sets the stage for a plethora of challenges in personal relationships and self-esteem.

Within the toxic family structure, emotional neglect ensures the perpetuation of unhealthy dynamics. Not only are the victims likely to struggle with acknowledging and expressing their emotions, but they may also repeat these patterns with their own children or in other close relationships, often without conscious awareness of doing so. The cycle of ignoring emotional needs continues, reinforcing the family's dysfunctional narrative.

Moreover, the invisibility of emotional neglect makes it particularly insidious. Physical abuse or overt verbal criticisms are recognizable and, thus, easier to confront and label as unacceptable. Emotional neglect, however, is often harder to pinpoint and define. It lurks behind what isn't said, what isn't done, leaving its victims grappling with something they can't quite name.

For families entrenched in this cycle, recognition of emotional needs becomes a foreign concept, leading to a widespread inability to foster emotional intelligence. Members of these families might struggle with empathy, both towards themselves and others, due to their own unmet emotional needs and the lack of modeling on how to address emotions healthily.

The silence around emotional experiences encourages isolation among family members. Each individual might silently wrestle with their feelings, perceiving the absence of an emotional dialogue as an indicator that their experiences are unrelatable, further estranging them from one another. This isolation deepens the chasm between family members, making genuine connections and healing more difficult to achieve.

Healing from emotional neglect and breaking its cycle demands a conscious, deliberate effort to validate and express feelings. It begins with acknowledging the validity of one's emotions and learning to communicate them. This process involves unlearning the implicit message that emotional needs are irrelevant or burdensome, and instead, fostering an environment where they are recognized and valued.

Creating spaces for open emotional expression within the family requires patience and understanding. It involves actively listening to and validating each other's experiences without judgment. For those who have endured emotional neglect, this can feel unnervingly vulnerable at first, but it is a crucial step towards forging healthier relationships.

Support systems play an invaluable role in this healing journey. Therapists, support groups, and understanding friends can provide the external validation that was missing, offering a mirror to reflect and affirm the individual's worth and emotional experiences. Through these supportive relationships, one can begin to internalize the belief that their feelings matter.

Educating oneself about emotional literacy is another essential step. Understanding the landscape of emotions, how they work, and their importance in our lives empowers individuals to take ownership of their emotional experiences. This education can shift the internal narrative from one of neglect to one of affirmation and self-compassion.

It's important to recognize that healing from emotional neglect is a journey that unfolds in its own time. There will be moments of breakthrough and periods of stagnation. However, each step taken towards recognizing and validating one's emotional world is a step away from the cycle of toxicity that neglect perpetuates.

Moreover, breaking free from this cycle is not just about individual healing but also about creating a legacy of emotional health for future generations. By addressing and healing emotional neglect, one can forge a new path that honors emotional awareness and empathy, disrupting the lineage of pain.

In pursuit of healing, embracing vulnerability becomes a strength. It's in vulnerability that true emotional connection and healing are found. This path requires courage and resilience, but it offers the freedom of living authentically and forming genuine, nourishing relationships.

Ultimately, understanding and confronting emotional neglect is pivotal in dismantling family toxicity. It's about shedding light on the silent, unseen wounds and nurturing them with patience, empathy, and love. For those embarking on this journey, it's a profound act of reclaiming not only their emotional health but also their intrinsic right to be seen, heard, and valued.

# Chapter 3:
# Identifying Toxic Parenting Patterns

In the journey to understand the landscape of our upbringing, recognizing toxic parenting patterns emerges as a beacon of insight, guiding us toward healing. Our exploration uncovers the subtle and not-so-subtle ways in which manipulation and control have woven their intricate webs, alongside both covert and overt forms of abuse, within the family structure. As we chart this terrain, it's essential to remember that these patterns are not reflections of our worth but rather indications of our parents' struggles with their own limitations and unresolved issues. Identifying these behaviors is a step towards liberation, providing a map to navigate our past experiences, understand their impact on our present, and empower us to craft a future defined not by toxicity, but by our resilience and desire for genuine, loving connections. This chapter aims to illuminate these patterns with clarity and compassion, offering a beacon of hope for those ready to emerge from the shadow of toxic influence, affirming that understanding is the first step towards healing and, ultimately, towards reclaiming the narrative of one's life.

## Manipulation and Control Strategies

Continuing from the exploration of toxic family dynamics, this section delves deeply into the intricate and often covert world of manipulation and control strategies wielded by toxic parents. Manipulation, in this context, is not just a random act of selfishness; it's a systematic approach used by emotionally immature or unavailable parents to meet their own needs, at the expense of their children's psychological well-being.

At the heart of manipulation is the need for control. Control, as we'll explore, is the lifeblood of the toxic parent. It manifests in various forms, from overt commands to subtle insinuations, designed to undermine the child's autonomy, self-esteem, and reality. This tactics can be bewildering, leaving children in a perpetual state of trying to appease an unappeasable parent.

One common strategy is *gaslighting*, a term borrowed from the classic film where a husband attempts to make his wife doubt her sanity. In familial settings, this translates to parents denying a child's reality, dismissing their feelings, or contradicting their perceptions, thereby instilling doubt. This psychological manipulation causes the child to question their own memory, perception, or judgment, leading to a crippling lack of confidence.

*Conditional love* is another powerful tool in the manipulator's arsenal. Here, the parent's affection or attention is contingent upon the child's compliance with their demands or expectations. Children under such conditions grow up believing that their value is tied to their usefulness or conformity to their parent's wishes, thus stunting their development into autonomous individuals.

Guilt-tripping is a tactic frequently used to control. It involves inducing guilt in someone, for the purpose of controlling their behavior. Toxic parents might remind children of the sacrifices they've made for them, thus obligating the child to comply with their wishes out of guilt or a sense of debt.

Isolation is a much subtler, but equally devastating, strategy. Here, the parent might limit the child's interactions with peers or other family members, often under the guise of protection or love. The underlying motive, however, is to keep the child dependent and under control.

Threats and intimidation are more overt forms of control. Whether through verbal threats or through more subtle implications of potential loss (of love, security, etc.), these tactics are meant to instill fear and compliance.

At times, manipulation can take on a more benign appearance, such as excessive care or overinvolvement in the child's life, often referred to as *enmeshment*. Here, the parent's life becomes unduly entangled with that of the child. The boundary between where the parent ends and the child begins becomes blurred, inhibiting the child's ability to develop their own identity, preferences, and life path.

Favoritism and triangulation create a dynamic where the parent pits siblings against one another or shows undue preference to one child over others, eroding sibling bonds and fostering an environment of competition and insecurity.

Victimization is a tactic where the parent portrays themselves as the victim of circumstances or of the child's behavior. This manipulation tactic shifts responsibility from the parent to the child, often leading to the child caretaking the parent at the expense of their own needs.

Lastly, unpredictability and inconsistency in behavior can be a manipulation strategy. By keeping the child on edge, not knowing what to expect, the parent maintains control through confusion and fear of potential negative outcomes. This lack of a stable, predictable environment is profoundly disorienting for children, impacting their sense of security and well-being.

Recognizing these manipulation and control strategies is the first step toward healing. It involves a process of unlearning the distorted beliefs and behaviors instilled by toxic parents and relearning healthier, more autonomous ways of relating to oneself and others.

Healing from these manipulative tactics requires acknowledging the pain and confusion they have caused. It's a journey of moving from a fragmented sense of self, marred by years of manipulation, toward a more whole, integrated self. This journey isn't easy, but it is filled with the potential for growth, self-discovery, and liberation.

Empowerment comes from understanding these manipulation tactics, not to foster resentment, but to move beyond them. By recognizing these patterns, individuals can start to reclaim their autonomy, self-worth, and the capacity to form healthier relationships.

In this empowerment lies the key to breaking the cycle of toxicity. It's about building a life that is not a reaction to the past but a conscious creation of a future based on one's own values, desires, and boundaries. It's about redefining what love, respect, and care truly mean, free from the distortions of manipulation and control.

As we move forward, let's remember that healing and empowerment are within reach. It's about taking one step at a time, knowing that each step takes us further away from the shadow of manipulation and control, and closer to the light of autonomy, freedom, and true self-expression.

## Covert and Overt Forms of Abuse

As we delve deeper into understanding the complex landscape of toxic parenting, it's crucial to recognize that abuse within the family can manifest in both overt and covert forms. Both are equally damaging, yet they operate differently, impacting the psyche and emotional well-being of individuals in unique ways. By shedding light on these dynamics, we aim to empower survivors to acknowledge their experiences and facilitate a journey toward healing.

Abuse, in its overt form, is often easier to identify. It includes physical acts of violence, explicit verbal assaults, or any clear, tangible actions that directly harm the individual. These behaviors can leave visible scars, serving as stark reminders of the trauma endured. However, acknowledging and confronting these painful truths is the first step towards reclaiming one's sense of self-worth and strength.

On the flip side, covert abuse operates under the radar, consisting of subtle manipulations, emotional neglect, and psychological tactics that undermine the victim's confidence and sense of reality. This form of abuse is insidious, often going unnoticed by those outside the immediate family circle, and sometimes even by the victims themselves. It's a silent poison that seeps into the very foundation of one's being, distorting self-image and impeding the ability to forge healthy relationships.

Gaslighting is a common tactic in covert abuse, where the abuser denies the victim's reality, making them question their perceptions and memory. This psychological manipulation fosters an environment of confusion and insecurity, trapping the victim in a cycle of self-doubt and isolation. Recognizing gaslighting for what it is—a deliberate attempt to destabilize and control—is a monumental step in breaking free from its grasp.

Emotional neglect, another facet of covert abuse, involves the consistent disregard for a child's emotional needs. This neglect can make individuals feel fundamentally unworthy of love and attention, echoing through their adult lives in various forms of self-sabotage and relationship difficulties. Understanding that this neglect was not a reflection of your value but rather a failure on the part of the caregiver is pivotal in healing these deep-seated wounds.

The impact of these forms of abuse on personal development cannot be overstated. Survivors might struggle with forming a coherent sense of identity, battling with issues of trust, self-esteem, and the perpetual feeling of being 'less than.' However, it's important to remember that these outcomes are not fixed. Just as a broken bone can mend, the psyche possesses a remarkable capacity for recovery.

Breaking the silence surrounding abuse is fundamentally empowering. Sharing your story, whether in therapy, through creative expression, or in support groups, can be a powerful catalyst for healing. It validates your experiences, affirming that what happened was real, it mattered, and it was not your fault. This external affirmation is a crucial step on the path to internal acceptance and healing.

Therapeutic approaches that focus on trauma can provide invaluable tools for understanding and processing these experiences. Techniques such as cognitive-behavioral therapy (CBT), eye movement desensitization and reprocessing (EMDR), and narrative therapy offer structured means to untangle the web of abuse, facilitating a reclamation of personal narrative and power.

Forging connections with others who have walked similar paths can also provide a sense of solidarity and mutual understanding that is deeply healing. Support groups and online forums dedicated to survivors of family abuse offer spaces where one's experiences are not just believed but deeply felt and shared by others. These communities can act as anchors, reminding individuals that they are not alone in their journey.

Self-care is a crucial component of the healing journey. Engaging in activities that nourish the soul, such as meditation, journaling, or physical exercise, can help rebuild the sense of self-worth that abuse seeks to destroy. Remember, acts of self-care are not selfish; they are acts of rebellion against the messages of unworthiness that abuse imparts.

Setting boundaries with those who have harmed us is both an act of self-preservation and a declaration of self-respect. It sends a clear message that the cycle of abuse ends here. While setting and maintaining these boundaries can be challenging, especially when it involves family, it is essential for protecting your emotional well-being and fostering healthy, respectful relationships.

Educating oneself about the dynamics of toxic family systems and the effects of abuse can also be empowering. Knowledge arms us with the understanding necessary to dismantle the false narratives imposed by abusers, replacing them with a framework that supports growth, self-compassion, and resilience.

As we navigate the path of healing, it's essential to cultivate patience and kindness towards ourselves. The journey is not linear; there will be setbacks and moments of doubt. However, each step forward, no matter how small, is a victory. It's a testament to your strength, your courage, and your unwavering commitment to reclaiming your life.

Ultimately, moving beyond overt and covert forms of abuse is a deeply personal and transformative process. It's a journey that not only involves confronting and healing from past traumas but also embracing the possibility of a future filled with joy, peace, and authentic connections. By recognizing and addressing these forms of abuse, we take the first steps towards breaking the cycle, paving the way for a legacy of love, respect, and emotional wellness.

In closing, remember that your experiences, while profoundly shaping you, do not define you. You are not the hurt inflicted upon you or the silence you were forced into. You are a being of immense worth, deserving of love and happiness. Stepping into this truth and owning your journey of recovery is perhaps the most powerful act of self-love and rebellion against the legacy of abuse.

# Chapter 4:
# The Legacy of Selfish Parental Behavior

The footprint of selfish behavior by parents on the sands of their children's development is deep and enduring, shaping their emotional landscape in complex and challenging ways. This legacy, often cloaked in normalized familial interactions, leaves indelible marks on the child's psyche, fostering a skewed perception of love, self-worth, and relational dynamics. The essence of selfishness in parenting—characterized by prioritizing one's own needs and desires at the expense of the child's emotional and psychological well-being—sets the stage for a myriad of developmental consequences. It's a terrain marked by the echoes of unmet needs, the shadows of conditional affection, and the thirst for genuine validation and support.

As we navigate through this chapter, we'll unravel the intricate web of self-centeredness in the parenting realm and its profound ripple effects on a child's development. Understanding the legacy of such behavior is a crucial step toward healing and growth. It's about acknowledging the pain, yes, but it's also about empowering ourselves to move beyond the confines of our upbringing. The journey through this recognition is not just a path of healing but also a testament to the resilience of the human spirit. Unraveling the complex legacy of selfish parental behavior holds the key to unlocking a deeper understanding of ourselves, fostering a nurturing self-relationship, and ultimately, paving the way for a brighter, more authentic future, unfettered by the shadows of the past.

## Self-Centeredness in Parenting

As we delve into exploring self-centeredness within the context of parenting, it's crucial to recognize how this trait not only shapes the dynamics within a family but profoundly impacts the emotional and psychological development of children. Self-centered parents, often consumed with their own needs, wishes, and feelings, might overlook or entirely disregard the needs of their children. This negligence, whether intentional or due to a lack of awareness, sows seeds of long-lasting issues that extend far into adulthood.

At its core, self-centeredness in parenting manifests as a fundamental failure to acknowledge and meet the emotional needs of the child. Such parents may prioritize their own desires and problems, viewing their children more as extensions of themselves rather than as independent individuals with their own set of needs, feelings, and aspirations. This skewed perspective not only stifles the child's emotional growth but also their ability to form a healthy sense of self.

Children raised by self-centered parents often wrestle with feelings of inadequacy and low self-esteem. When a parent's attention is perennially fixated on their own needs, children may internalize the notion that their needs are unimportant or, even worse, burdensome. This belief can lead to a lifelong struggle with asserting oneself and seeking validation in unfulfilling ways.

The dynamics of a family influenced by self-centered parenting can also cultivate an environment where emotional expression is discouraged or outright ignored. Children learn early on that expressing their feelings does not elicit a supportive response but rather, might inconvenience or upset their parent. This conditioning discourages openness and can significantly hinder emotional intelligence, interpersonal skills, and the capacity to form healthy relationships later in life.

Moreover, self-centeredness in parenting often equates to inconsistent emotional availability. Moments of warmth and affection may be fleeting, entirely contingent on the parent's mood or needs at the time. This inconsistency can deeply confuse and hurt a child, fostering a sense of insecurity and distrust in relationships that can persist into adulthood.

It's also imperative to acknowledge the role of manipulation in self-centered parenting. Parents might employ guilt, shame, or even affection as tools to mold their child's behavior to their own liking, further entrenching the belief in children that they must earn love and affection through compliance and sacrificing their own needs.

Dealing with the legacy of self-centered parenting requires a multifaceted approach that begins with awareness. Recognizing and acknowledging the ways in which one's upbringing has influenced their beliefs, behaviors, and emotional responses, is the first step towards healing. Validation of one's experiences and feelings is crucial in dismantling the deep-seated notion that one's needs are unimportant or invalid.

Healing from such a legacy also involves relearning one's worth outside the confines of performance or compliance. It's about realizing that your value is not contingent on catering to the needs of others, especially at the expense of your own health and happiness. This realization paves the way for asserting boundaries, a skill often underdeveloped in those raised by self-centered parents. Establishing and maintaining boundaries is vital in reclaiming autonomy over one's emotional well-being.

Sometimes, the road to recovery may include seeking therapeutic support. A therapist can provide the safe space required to unpack and understand the complexities of one's upbringing. Through therapy, individuals can learn healthier ways of relating to themselves and others, strategies for managing difficult emotions, and techniques for rebuilding a stronger, more positive self-image.

It's equally important to foster relationships that model healthy dynamics. Surrounding oneself with individuals who respect boundaries, communicate openly, and reciprocate emotional support can offer valuable learning experiences and reassurance of one's worth and capabilities.

Embracing self-care is another essential component in healing from self-centered parenting. Self-care is an affirmation of one's worth and a fundamental practice in setting and honoring one's boundaries. It encompasses not just physical care but also attending to one's emotional and psychological needs—a concept often neglected in homes dominated by self-centered parenting.

Lastly, advocacy and raising awareness about toxic family dynamics play a significant role not just in personal healing but in societal change. By sharing personal stories and supporting others on their healing journey, survivors contribute to a culture that recognizes and addresses the impacts of toxic parenting, promoting healthier family dynamics for future generations.

Self-centeredness in parenting, with its complex implications and far-reaching effects, presents a significant challenge to the emotional well-being of children. However, it is important to remember that its legacy, while profound, is not unalterable. Through awareness, therapeutic intervention, and a commitment to personal growth, individuals can navigate the path to healing and reclaim a sense of self that is defined not by past neglect but by their own inherent worth and capacity for love and connection.

Understanding and healing from the wounds of self-centered parenting is not only a deeply personal journey but also a powerful statement of resilience and self-compassion. As we move forward, let us embrace the strength that lies in vulnerability, the power of self-awareness, and the promise of a future shaped by our own hands—free from the shadows of the past.

## Consequences for the Child's Development

As we explore this crucial aspect, it is important to understand the profound impact that self-centered parenting can have on a child's development. The behaviors exhibited by parents who are more concerned with their own needs than those of their children create ripples that extend far into the future, shaping the psyche, emotional health, and relational abilities of their offspring.

One of the most significant consequences for children growing up in such an environment is the development of low self-esteem. When parents prioritize their own needs and desires, often at the expense of acknowledging and celebrating their child's achievements and milestones, it sends a powerful message to the child that they are not valuable or worthy of attention. This can result in a deep-seated belief in their own inadequacy, which can hinder personal growth and the pursuit of their aspirations.

Another fallout from this dynamic is the struggle with boundaries. Children raised by self-centered parents may never learn to set healthy boundaries, as their own needs were consistently sidelined. This can lead to problems in asserting themselves in relationships, workplaces, and other social settings, potentially leading to a pattern of being taken advantage of or neglecting their own needs.

Children from such backgrounds often develop an anxious or avoidant attachment style, based on the unpredictable levels of attention and affection received from their parents. This can affect their future relationships, making it difficult for them to form secure and trusting bonds with others. The inconsistency of emotional support received at home may drive them to either cling to relationships out of fear of abandonment or keep others at arm's length to avoid getting hurt.

There can also be an exaggerated fear of failure among these individuals. Growing up with self-centered parents who may have dismissed or harshly criticized mistakes can instill a paralyzing fear of making errors. This fear can inhibit taking necessary risks or trying new things, stifling creativity and personal exploration.

Moreover, children of self-centered parents often experience difficulty in recognizing and expressing their emotions. They might have grown up in an environment where expressing feelings was discouraged or ignored, leading to challenges in emotional regulation and expression in adulthood. This emotional suppression can contribute to mental health issues such as anxiety and depression.

Ironically, some children of self-centered parents become overly empathetic to the needs of others, at the expense of their own. Constantly attuned to the moods and desires of their parents, they may lose sight of their own needs and desires. While empathy is a valuable trait, when it comes at the expense of one's own well-being, it can lead to burnout and resentment.

Furthermore, trust issues are a common consequence. Growing up in an environment where the primary caregivers were unreliable or dismissive can lead to a deep-seated mistrust of others' intentions. This skepticism can make forming meaningful connections challenging, as there's always a fear that others will disappoint or exploit them.

Academically and professionally, the impact of a self-centered upbringing can manifest in perfectionism or a chronic lack of motivation. The former may be driven by a desire to finally gain the approval of their parents by being perfect, while the latter could stem from a deeply ingrained belief that they are incapable of succeeding.

Moreover, individuals raised in such environments might find themselves replicating the toxic dynamics in their own relationships, continuing the cycle of dysfunction. Unlearning these patterns requires a conscious effort and often, professional help.

Navigating adulthood, individuals from such backgrounds might feel a pervasive sense of loneliness, stemming from the isolation experienced in their formative years. Building a genuine connection with others can seem daunting when one's upbringing lacked warmth and understanding.

In terms of health, chronic stress from navigating a toxic familial environment can lead to both short-term and long-lasting physical health issues. The constant vigilance and stress can impact the immune system, lead to sleep disturbances, and even chronic conditions like heart disease.

However, it's crucial to note that the consequences of growing up under the shadow of self-centered parents, while significant, do not dictate one's fate. Recognition and acknowledgment of these patterns is the first step towards healing and growth. Many find strength in their experiences, using them as a catalyst for building a life that is rich in empathy, understanding, and genuine connections.

Support from therapists, self-help resources, and a compassionate community can play a pivotal role in navigating the journey of recovery. Embracing vulnerability and seeking to understand oneself deeply can unlock doors to profound personal development and fulfilling relationships.

In wrapping up this exploration, it's clear that while the consequences for a child's development stemming from self-centered parental behavior are far-reaching and multifaceted, they also illuminate the path to resilience and transformation. These challenges, once recognized, offer unparalleled opportunities for growth, self-awareness, and the ability to sculpt a life defined not by the past but by the possibilities of the future.

# Chapter 5:
# Breaking the Cycle: Recognizing Red Flags

After uncovering the deep-seated issues that toxic parenting leaves in its wake, it's crucial to pivot towards a brighter path by breaking the cycle. This chapter leans into the first step of that journey: recognizing the red flags that indicate a continuation of toxic patterns in adult relationships. Imagine walking through a dense forest, the trees are the people and situations in your life, and you're looking for signs that guide you to clear, open spaces. That's what identifying red flags is all about. Just like seedlings that mirror the ancient trees, patterns that echo toxic family behavior in our adult relationships often start small—subtle comments, occasional disregard for boundaries, or slight manipulations. These early warning signs are the universe's way of nudging us, urging us to pay attention before we find ourselves in a thicket of thorns. But how do we discern a mere sapling from a benign plant? It's about tuning into our intuition, learning from our past, and applying those lessons to our present and future. By recognizing these early signs, we create a momentous opportunity: the possibility to steer clear of environments and relationships that replicate the toxicity we once knew all too well. This chapter doesn't just highlight the problem areas; it's a blueprint for cultivating awareness and fostering the courage to trust yourself. It's time we break the cycle by acknowledging the red flags waving in our peripheral vision, empowering us to choose a different path—one that leads to genuine connections, self-respect, and ultimately, healing.

## Early Warning Signs of Toxic Relationships

As we journey through life, the relationships we foster can either uplift us or weigh us down. Recognizing the early warning signs of toxic relationships is paramount in protecting our emotional well-being. This wisdom becomes even more crucial for those of us who are navigating the world after surviving toxic family dynamics. It's about understanding that certain unsettling patterns we witnessed or experienced in our familial relationships can reappear in our interactions outside the family unit.

One such sign is the feeling of being consistently undermined or devalued. If you notice that your opinions are regularly dismissed or ridiculed in a relationship, it's a red flag. This behavior can create an environment where your self-esteem is continuously eroded, making you doubt your worth and abilities. It's a pattern familiar to those who have endured toxic upbringing, where one's feelings and thoughts were often negated.

Another early warning is the imbalance of power. Relationships should be partnerships where both parties have equal say and respect. A toxic relationship often has an uneven distribution of power, where one person's needs and demands overshadow the other's. This dynamic can feel eerily similar to childhood experiences under authoritative or controlling parents, where autonomy was stifled.

Excessive jealousy or possessiveness is also a hallmark of toxicity. While it's natural for partners to feel a degree of jealousy at times, it becomes unhealthy when it leads to controlling behaviors or invasions of privacy. Such actions reflect a lack of trust and security within the relationship, often mirroring the lack of emotional safety felt in toxic familial environments.

Communication in any healthy relationship should be open, honest, and respectful. A relationship veering toward toxicity often features communication that's filled with criticism, sarcasm, or contempt. It's crucial to recognize these patterns early on. They're corrosive to emotional connection and respect, closely mirroring the communication breakdowns experienced in toxic family settings.

A sense of walking on eggshells, feeling like you have to constantly monitor your words or actions to avoid conflict, indicates a relationship steeped in anxiety and fear, not love and respect. It echoes the unpredictability and tension characteristic of growing up in a toxic household.

Isolation is another significant warning sign. A toxic partner may attempt to cut you off from your support network, making you more dependent on them and easier to control. It's a tactic that's painfully familiar to those who have dealt with manipulative family members.

Furthermore, if you find yourself making excuses for your partner's harmful behavior or if you're often the one apologizing after every argument, it's time to pause and reflect. This pattern of rationalizing abuse and taking responsibility for conflicts, regardless of fault, is something many survivors of toxic upbringing know all too well.

When affection or kindness is weaponized, it's a strategy of control, not genuine care. If warmth and love are only offered conditionally, based on your compliance or performance, it's a manipulative tactic, not unlike the conditional love received from emotionally immature or manipulative parents.

Additionally, one's inability to express their true self without fear of judgment or repercussion is indicative of a toxic relationship. Authentic relationships encourage and celebrate individuality and personal growth, contrasting sharply with toxic environments where conformity and submission are often demanded.

A partner who refuses to acknowledge your feelings or perspective, insisting instead on their version of events or dismissing your concerns, is engaging in gaslighting. This form of psychological manipulation is damaging and disorienting, much like the confusion sown by toxic parents denying or trivializing your emotions.

Lastly, the perpetual cycle of highs followed by explosive lows, promises of change followed by inevitable disappointment, creates an addictive toxicity. This dynamic, akin to the unpredictable moods and promises of toxic parents, can leave one perpetually hoping for change that never fully materializes.

Recognizing these early warning signs is the first step toward protecting oneself from further emotional harm. It enables us to make informed choices about the relationships we choose to nurture and those we decide to let go. The goal is not only to prevent the perpetuation of toxic dynamics but to actively seek out relationships that are healthy, uplifting, and empowering.

Empowerment comes from understanding that you deserve to be treated with respect, kindness, and love — both from yourself and others. Moving beyond the shadow of toxic upbringing involves redefining what it means to be in a healthy relationship and knowing that it's possible to break the cycle of toxicity. It begins with valuing your well-being, setting boundaries, and not settling for relationships that echo the pain of the past.

It's about creating a life where relationships are a source of strength, growth, and joy. Recognizing and addressing the early warning signs of toxic relationships is an essential part of the journey toward healing and empowerment. The path may not always be smooth, but with awareness and self-compassion, it's possible to cultivate relationships that truly enrich your life.

## Patterns That Mirror Toxic Family Behavior

In this section, we delve into the subtle, often unrecognized ways that toxic family dynamics can persist and manifest in various aspects of adult life. Identifying these patterns is a crucial step towards healing and breaking the cycle of toxicity. Much like a shadow that follows on a sunny day, the influence of a toxic upbringing can stretch far into an individual's future, shaping their relationships, self-esteem, and even their parenting style.

Toxic family behaviors often leave a latent template, guiding how individuals view themselves and the world around them. It's not uncommon for adult children of toxic parents to find themselves in relationships that eerily echo the dynamics of their upbringing. This isn't a mere coincidence but a reflection of an ingrained pattern of thinking and being that was normalized during their formative years.

One clear sign of this mirroring is in the choice of romantic partners who, on some level, replicate the emotional unavailability or manipulative behaviors experienced in childhood. It's as if the familiarity of these dynamics breeds a misplaced comfort, a comfort that unfortunately comes with a heavy cost to one's well-being and happiness.

Another arena where these mirrored behaviors manifest is in boundary-setting, or rather, the lack thereof. Growing up in an environment where personal boundaries were either not respected or outright ignored teaches individuals that their needs and limits don't hold value. As a result, they may struggle to assert themselves in personal and professional relationships, perpetuating a cycle of neglect and exploitation.

Work environments can also reflect familial patterns of toxicity. Individuals may subconsciously gravitate towards high-stress roles or workplaces that replicate the chaos and unpredictability of their family home. Here, the cycle of tension and relief mirrors the unpredictable moods they navigated as children, reinforcing a sense of normalcy in dysfunction.

Frequent self-doubt and harsh self-criticism can be telltale vestiges of a toxic upbringing. These individuals often internalize the negative messages received during childhood, leading to an inner monologue that is unforgiving and unkind. This punitive self-talk not only undermines self-esteem but also reinforces the belief that they are deserving of poor treatment by others.

Control tactics learned in childhood may manifest in subtle or overt ways. Some may find themselves engaging in manipulative behaviors to elicit certain responses or outcomes from others, replicating the only influence tactics they saw modeled. Recognizing and unlearning these patterns is essential for fostering healthy, authentic connections.

Over-responsibility for others' feelings and outcomes is another common pattern. Growing up in a toxic family often means learning to preempt and manage the emotional states of others at the expense of one's own needs. In adulthood, this can translate into co-dependent relationships where the individual constantly places others' needs above their own, perpetuating a cycle of self-neglect.

Risk aversion and a fear of failure can be significantly heightened in those with toxic familial backgrounds. The high stakes attached to mistakes or failure in the toxic family environment create a paralyzing fear of taking risks. This fear can limit personal and professional growth, as individuals shy away from opportunities that carry even the slightest risk of failure.

Conversely, some individuals may swing to the opposite extreme, engaging in risk-taking behaviors as a form of rebellion against the tightly controlled environment of their upbringing. This pendulum swing, while seemingly opposite, is equally a reflection of unresolved childhood dynamics and a search for identity and autonomy outside of those toxic patterns.

Perhaps one of the most poignant reflections of toxic family behavior is in the realm of parenting. Many individuals vow not to repeat their parents' mistakes, yet find themselves struggling with the same patterns of behavior. The immense pressure of breaking the cycle can sometimes lead to overcorrection or, conversely, a replication of learned behavior. Awareness, patience, and support are crucial in navigating this journey.

The road to healing and breaking the cycle of toxic family behaviors is fraught with challenges but is undeniably rewarding. Recognizing these mirrored patterns is the first step towards change. It requires courage to confront and unlearn the deeply ingrained behaviors that have subtly directed one's life.

Embracing vulnerability, seeking supportive relationships, and engaging in personal growth endeavors can illuminate the path forward. We are not our past, and the cycle of toxicity stops with us. It's about forging a new path that honors our experiences but is not defined by them.

Empowerment comes from understanding that we have the choice and power to redefine our narrative. It's an invitation to step into our authenticity, celebrate our resilience, and cultivate the life we deserve—one of fulfillment, love, and joy, free from the shadows of toxicity.

The journey of healing and empowerment is a testament to the strength and resilience of the human spirit. It is a profound act of self-love to reclaim our lives from the grips of toxic family behavior. Let this knowledge be a beacon of hope and a guide as we navigate the complexities of redefining our sense of self and relationships. Our past does not dictate our future; with awareness, support, and determination, we can break free from the patterns that once held us back and step into a brighter, healthier future.

# Chapter 6:
# Setting Boundaries with Toxic Family Members

As we dive into the heart of reclaiming our sense of self from the grips of toxic family dynamics, we're confronted with the paramount challenge and necessity of setting boundaries. The journey to healing is not just about recognizing the pain inflicted by toxic family members but bravely asserting our right to protect our peace. Establishing boundaries isn't an act of defiance but a profound declaration of self-respect and love. It's acknowledging that while we can't change the past or control others' actions, we have the power to dictate the terms of our engagement with those who've hurt us.

At the core of this transformative process is the understanding that boundaries are not walls built from resentment or anger, but fences laced with compassion—both for ourselves and, if we choose, for those who've wronged us. It involves clearly communicating our needs, limits, and expectations in a manner that's assertive but not aggressive, ensuring that our emotional well-being is shielded from further harm. This chapter will guide you through identifying when and where to draw these lines, how to maintain them amidst pushback, and why your recovery depends on this crucial step. It's about equipping you with effective strategies to not only articulate what you will and will not tolerate but also to enforce these parameters without guilt or second-guessing.

Remember, setting boundaries is an essential step towards healing, as it fosters a healthy environment where our self-esteem can thrive. It teaches us that saying 'no' to what diminishes us is, in fact, saying 'yes' to ourselves—to our recovery, our worth, and our unapologetic pursuit of happiness. Embrace this journey of boundary-setting with an understanding heart and a steadfast resolve, knowing that it paves the way for a future where you are no longer defined by your past, but by the strength and resilience with which you've reclaimed your life.

## The Importance of Boundaries for Self-Protection

As we navigate through the arduous journey of healing from the wounds inflicted by toxic parents, one of the most vital tools at our disposal is the establishment of boundaries. Boundaries serve as a critical form of self-protection, enabling us to safeguard our mental, emotional, and physical well-being. This section delves into the importance of setting boundaries for individuals who have endured the challenges of being raised in an environment characterized by toxic parenting. Through the lens of empathy, motivation, and inspiration, we will explore how boundaries are not just barriers but are, in fact, crucial for asserting our worth and initiating the journey to reclaim our lives.

Boundaries, in essence, are the invisible lines we draw around ourselves to define what is and isn't acceptable behavior from others. For those who have grown up in toxic family dynamics, the concept of boundaries might be unfamiliar or even unsettling. It's not uncommon for survivors to feel guilt or apprehension at the thought of setting limits with their family members. However, it's imperative to recognize that healthy boundaries are not about creating conflict; they are about cultivating respect.

Boundaries help in delineating where we end and others begin. For adult children of toxic parents, realizing that they have the right to their own feelings, thoughts, and needs is a significant breakthrough. Establishing boundaries is akin to saying, "I am worthy of respect, and my needs matter." This realization is a powerful statement in the journey towards self-healing and empowerment.

The process of setting boundaries might evoke fear of retaliation or rejection from toxic family members. It's important to understand that setting boundaries is not an act of aggression but rather an act of self-respect. When done with a clear mind and a compassionate heart, establishing boundaries can serve as a pivotal step in breaking the cycle of toxicity and enabling personal growth.

Toxic parenting often involves manipulation, emotional blackmail, or complete disregard for personal space. In such environments, children grow up without a clear understanding of personal boundaries. As adults, this can translate into difficulty in saying no, people-pleasing behavior, and an overarching sense of being lost in the needs and wants of others. Recognizing these patterns is the first step towards change.

Setting boundaries requires courage, clarity, and consistency. It starts with identifying your limits—understanding what you can tolerate and what makes you uncomfortable or hurt. This is a deeply personal process and requires introspection and honesty with oneself. Once you know your boundaries, communicating them clearly and respectfully to those around you is the next step.

Resistance from toxic family members is common when one starts to set boundaries. They may react with anger, guilt-tripping, or even mockery. It's essential to stay firm, remind yourself why you're setting these boundaries, and seek support from friends, therapists, or support groups. Remember, setting boundaries is not about changing others' behavior but about protecting yourself.

One might worry that setting boundaries means cutting people out of their life entirely. While in some cases, distancing might be necessary for one's well-being, in others, boundaries can simply mean limiting exposure to toxic behavior, or deciding what topics are off-limits. The key is to customize your boundaries to align with your values, needs, and the level of toxicity you're dealing with.

It's also crucial to set boundaries with oneself. This includes recognizing self-critical thoughts, setting limits on self-sacrificing behaviors, and prioritizing self-care. Often, we are our own harshest critics, especially when coming from a background of toxic parenting. Learning to be kind and compassionate to oneself is a transformative aspect of healing.

Beyond protection, setting boundaries grants us the freedom to discover who we are outside of our toxic family dynamics. It allows us the space to explore our interests, beliefs, and values without the overshadowing influence of toxic parental figures. This discovery is essential in building a life that feels genuinely our own.

Moreover, by asserting our boundaries, we teach others how to treat us. This not only aids in deterring toxic behavior but also attracts healthier, more respectful relationships into our lives. People start to respect our needs and space, and we learn to reciprocate, fostering mutual respect and understanding.

In navigating the journey of setting boundaries, remember that setbacks and challenges are part of the process. There may be times when you falter, and that's okay. What's important is that you keep moving forward, learning from each experience, and continuously advocating for your well-being.

The journey of healing from the fallout of toxic parenting is arduous and fraught with challenges. However, establishing boundaries is a beacon of hope on this journey. It's a testament to the fact that you are taking back control of your life, one step at a time. It's a profound affirmation of your worthiness, your strength, and your capacity to break the cycle of toxicity.

As you embrace this journey, understand that the path to healing is not linear. Each step you take towards establishing boundaries is a step towards reclaiming your life and discovering the boundless potential within you. Remember, you are deserving of respect, love, and a life that is fully your own. Let setting boundaries be your shield and your declaration of self-love and self-respect as you navigate through the healing process.

In summary, boundaries are not just about keeping others out. They are about letting ourselves in - into a life of self-respect, growth, and genuine happiness. As survivors of toxic parents, learning to set these boundaries is crucial for our self-protection and our ultimate healing. It's a journey worth undertaking, filled with challenges, certainly, but also with immense rewards.

## Effective Strategies for Establishing and Maintaining Boundaries

As we delve into the heart of establishing and maintaining boundaries with toxic family members, it's vital to acknowledge that this process is both a form of self-preservation and a step towards healing. Boundaries are not walls meant to isolate us but rather guidelines that help us interact with others in a way that preserves our well-being. In this journey, we will explore strategies that empower you to set healthy boundaries, ensuring that your progress towards healing and empowerment remains steadfast.

First, understanding what boundaries are and are not, is crucial. Boundaries are not a means of manipulating or controlling others but are assertions of your needs and limits. They serve as a declaration of what you consider acceptable and unacceptable in your interactions with others. It's about respecting yourself enough to say, "I deserve to be treated with respect and dignity, and here's what that looks like for me."

Begin by reflecting on areas of your life where boundaries might be needed. This reflection involves identifying past instances where you felt disrespected, violated, or drained. Was it during conversations about personal life choices, or perhaps around financial matters? Pinpointing these areas provides a clear direction on where to start setting boundaries.

Communicating your boundaries is next, and it's often the most challenging part. Approach this conversation with clarity and calmness, focusing on "I" statements to express how certain behaviors affect you and what you need instead. This method reduces defensiveness and keeps the focus on your feelings and needs.

Expect resistance. Toxic individuals may not respect your boundaries initially because they are not used to being held accountable. Stay firm, and remember that your self-respect is not up for negotiation. This might mean having to repeat your stance more than once or even reducing contact if your boundaries continue to be disregarded.

Practice consistency. The effectiveness of boundaries relies on your consistency. If you're inconsistent, it sends a mixed message that your boundaries aren't serious and can be overlooked. Remember, it's okay to adjust your boundaries as you grow, but make sure these adjustments are truly reflective of your needs and not a concession to someone else's disregard for your limits.

Seek support. Establishing boundaries can be emotionally taxing, especially when dealing with pushback. Surround yourself with friends, family, or a therapist who understands your journey and can offer encouragement when things get tough.

Use affirmative self-talk. Remind yourself regularly of your right to set boundaries. Positive affirmations like "I am worthy of respect and kindness" can fortify your resolve and remind you why setting boundaries is essential for your mental health and well-being.

Recognize and celebrate your progress. Acknowledge the courage it takes to establish and maintain boundaries. Celebrating even the small victories can bolster your confidence and motivate you to keep going, even when it's challenging.

Learn to say no. This two-letter word is incredibly powerful in boundary-setting. Saying no is a complete sentence and requires no explanation. It's a fundamental right to decline situations or demands that don't align with your well-being.

Understand that boundary setting is an act of self-love. It's not selfish to prioritize your health and happiness. You're not responsible for how others react to your boundaries. You are only responsible for communicating them respectfully and clearly.

Visualize your boundaries. Sometimes, visualizing a physical barrier can help reinforce your mental and emotional boundaries. This mental imagery can be a helpful reminder that you are protected and in control of your own space and interactions.

Be patient with yourself. Setting boundaries is a skill that takes time to develop. There might be setbacks, but each attempt is a step forward in your journey towards a healthier, more empowered self.

Finally, embrace the freedom that comes with boundaries. While the process can be fraught with challenges, the liberation you'll feel from no longer being subject to toxic dynamics is immensely rewarding. Boundaries allow you to engage in relationships on your terms, fostering a sense of peace and autonomy.

In conclusion, establishing and maintaining boundaries with toxic family members is a critical step in healing from an upbringing marked by toxicity. It enables you to reclaim your power and chart a course towards a life defined by respect, self-love, and genuine connections.

Remember, you're not alone on this journey. With each boundary set, you're paving a new path towards a more fulfilling life, free from the shadows of negativity.

# Chapter 7:
# Healing from Emotional Scars

The journey of healing from the emotional scars left by a toxic upbringing is both challenging and rewarding. It requires a deep commitment to understanding oneself, the courage to face painful memories, and the resilience to rebuild from the inside out. As we navigate this path, it's crucial to acknowledge that healing isn't a linear process—it ebbs and flows, with setbacks and breakthroughs. Embracing this journey means accepting where we are and understanding that healing is possible, even when it feels out of reach. Various therapeutic approaches can provide guidance and support through this healing process. From conventional psychotherapy to more holistic methods, each offers unique tools to help unravel the complex tapestry of our past trauma. What's important is finding what resonates with us, what nurtures our spirit, and what gives us a sense of progress. The act of healing is an act of reclaiming our lives, piece by piece, until we construct a new narrative of empowerment and resilience. It's about slowly removing the layers of pain to uncover the authentic self beneath, who's been waiting to shine all along. This chapter will explore not just the importance of embracing the healing process but also the therapeutic paths that can support us in moving beyond our emotional scars toward a place of strength and renewal.

## Embracing the Healing Process

Through the journey we have embarked upon together, we've explored the complex and often painful reality of toxic family dynamics.

Recognizing the impact of such environments is the first step. The next, perhaps equally challenging, is embracing the healing process—a journey not just of recovery but of profound transformation.

Healing from emotional scars inflicted by toxic parenting involves a multifaceted approach. It's not merely about moving past the pain but also understanding and then rewriting the narrative of one's life. It requires patience, self-compassion, and often guidance from professionals who can navigate these tender waters with care.

The idea of healing can sometimes feel daunting. Yet, it's essential to remember that it is a process, one that is non-linear and uniquely personal. The timeline varies for everyone, and setbacks do not equate to failure. They are, instead, part of the journey toward self-discovery and renewal.

Initially, the process may involve confronting and accepting the reality of one's experiences. Denial can be a strong barrier to healing; breaking through it requires courage and the willingness to face one's past. This step is not about assigning blame but acknowledging the facts of one's upbringing and its impacts.

Self-reflection plays a critical role in the healing process. Through it, we begin to identify the coping mechanisms we've adopted, perhaps unknowingly, in response to toxic family dynamics. Some of these mechanisms may have served as necessary shields but might no longer be beneficial or might even be detrimental to one's current well-being and relationships.

Fostering self-compassion is crucial. Survivors often harbor feelings of inadequacy or self-blame. It's important to recognize these feelings but not let them define one's self-worth. Practicing self-compassion means treating oneself with the same kindness and understanding one would offer a dear friend.

Seeking therapy can be a powerful step in the healing process. A skilled therapist can provide the safe space needed to explore painful memories and emotions. They can offer insights and coping strategies that might not be apparent when navigating this terrain alone. Therapy can take various forms, and finding the right approach and therapist is vital.

Creating boundaries is another essential aspect of healing. This might involve setting limits with toxic family members or choosing to limit contact. Establishing boundaries is a way to protect one's emotional well-being and assert one's autonomy.

Reclamation of one's identity is a profound aspect of the healing journey. Toxic upbringing can profoundly impact one's sense of self. Healing allows for the exploration and discovery of who one is outside of the family drama—recognizing and embracing one's values, beliefs, and aspirations.

Building a supportive network plays a significant role in healing. Surrounding oneself with caring, understanding individuals who affirm your experiences and worth can be incredibly empowering. This network can include friends, chosen family, support groups, or a therapeutic community.

Engaging in self-care activities is another healing aspect. Self-care can take many forms, from physical activities that boost one's health to creative expressions that provide an outlet for emotions. The key is finding what resonates and brings joy and balance.

Forgiveness, a personal and complex decision, may come up in the healing journey. It's important to note that forgiveness is for the survivor's peace and does not condone or excuse the toxic behavior. The timing and capacity for forgiveness vary greatly, and it's a path that can only be chosen by the individual.

Throughout the healing process, celebrating small victories is essential. Acknowledging progress, no matter how minor it might seem, fosters a sense of accomplishment and encourages continued growth. Celebrations serve as reminders of one's strength and resilience.

Lastly, embracing the healing process means accepting that it is both an end and a beginning. While one part of the journey is overcoming the effects of toxic parenting, another equally important part is the ongoing process of growth, self-discovery, and creating a life filled with meaning and joy.

The path of healing from the scars of toxic parenting is not easy, but it is immeasurably rewarding. It opens up possibilities for a life unencumbered by the past—a life where one can thrive, not in spite of the challenges faced, but because of the strength gained in overcoming them. Embracing the healing process is a testament to the human spirit's resilience and capacity for renewal. It's a journey well worth taking.

## Therapeutic Approaches to Addressing Past Trauma

The journey towards healing from the wounds of toxic parenting is often arduous and deeply personal. For many, it involves confronting painful memories and breaking free from the hold of the past. Therapeutic interventions can play a critical role in this process, offering a beacon of hope and a roadmap towards emotional freedom. This section explores various therapeutic approaches that have been shown to be effective in addressing past trauma, particularly that stemming from toxic family dynamics.

One of the foundational approaches in addressing past traumas is cognitive-behavioral therapy (CBT). CBT helps individuals understand the interplay between their thoughts, feelings, and behaviors. It's particularly effective in challenging and changing unhelpful beliefs and thought patterns that have been internalized as a result of toxic parenting. By focusing on altering present behaviors and thoughts, CBT can empower survivors to break free from the chains of their past, promoting healing and resilience.

Another valuable approach is dialectical behavior therapy (DBT), which emphasizes the development of coping skills to manage emotions, improve relationships, and live more mindfully. Particularly for those who have experienced emotional neglect or instability, DBT's focus on emotional regulation and distress tolerance can be life-changing. The therapeutic environment fosters a sense of understanding and acceptance, vital for individuals who've often felt misunderstood and rejected.

Psychodynamic therapy is another pathway through which individuals can explore the root causes of their trauma. This approach delves into how early life experiences, particularly with toxic parents, influence present emotions and behaviors. It's a journey towards self-awareness, allowing individuals to understand and heal from their childhood wounds, thus enabling them to form healthier relationships in adulthood.

Eye Movement Desensitization and Reprocessing (EMDR) therapy has emerged as a particularly effective treatment for trauma. EMDR helps individuals process and integrate traumatic memories in a way that diminishes their power. For survivors of toxic parenting, this can mean the difference between being controlled by past experiences and moving forward with one's life. The therapy's structured approach fosters a sense of safety, essential for healing.

Art and expressive therapies offer a unique avenue for confronting and healing from past trauma. Through artistic expression, individuals can communicate feelings and experiences that might be too difficult to verbalize. This form of therapy validates the individual's experience and fosters a sense of creativity and empowerment, crucial for those who've been made to feel powerless in their family environments.

Narrative Therapy is another empowering approach. It helps individuals re-author their life stories, shifting the narrative from one of victimhood and suffering to one of resilience and agency. This therapeutic process enables survivors to see themselves as separate from their trauma, giving them the space to rewrite their futures.

Furthermore, mindfulness and meditation practices have proven to be invaluable in the healing process. They teach survivors to anchor themselves in the present, fostering a sense of peace and detachment from the turbulence of their past experiences. These practices can improve emotional regulation and reduce symptoms of anxiety and depression, common among those dealing with past trauma.

Support groups and therapy groups also offer significant benefits, providing a sense of community and shared experience. They stand as a powerful reminder that one is not alone in their struggles. These groups offer both support and perspective, as members share stories of pain and triumph, collectively fostering an environment of healing and understanding.

Family therapy can also play a crucial role, especially when there's a desire or necessity to maintain relationships with family members. It seeks to improve communication and resolve conflicts, facilitating a healthier dynamic. Though not always possible or desired in the context of toxic family relationships, when viable, it can lead to profound healing and reconciliation.

Somatic experiencing is a therapeutic approach focused on the body's role in trauma. It helps individuals tune into their bodily sensations and gently work through the trauma stored within their bodies. This can be particularly effective for those whose traumatic experiences have left them disconnected from their bodies or laden with unexplained physical symptoms.

Integration of these therapeutic approaches, tailored to an individual's specific needs and history, can facilitate a holistic path to healing. It's about finding what resonates and works for an individual, as there's no one-size-fits-all solution to healing from trauma. The process is often non-linear, marked by setbacks and breakthroughs. Yet, with persistence and the right support, moving beyond the trauma of toxic parenting is very much within reach.

The decision to seek therapy is a powerful step towards healing. It's an acknowledgment of one's worth and the belief in the possibility of a brighter, healthier future. It requires courage to confront the past and the determination to forge a new path forward.

It's essential to select a therapist or therapeutic approach that feels right. This might mean trying out different therapists or modalities until finding the right fit. Healing is a deeply personal journey, and the therapeutic relationship is its cornerstone. Trust, understanding, and connection with one's therapist are paramount.

Lastly, patience with oneself throughout the therapeutic journey cannot be overstated. Healing from the trauma of toxic parenting takes time and self-compassion. There will be moments of pain and resistance, but also moments of profound insight and liberation. It's a journey back to oneself, a reclamation of one's identity, and the construction of a life not defined by the past. The path forward is one of hope, resilience, and renewal.

# Chapter 8:
# Reclaiming Your Life: Strategies and Tools

Emerging from the shadow of a toxic upbringing can at times feel like navigating through a dense fog—uncertain and disorienting. Yet, within this chapter, you'll find a beacon to guide you towards reclaiming your life. It's time to shift the focus inward, prioritizing self-care not as an indulgence, but as an act of resistance against the past's hold on your present. Embracing self-compassion and nurturing your physical, emotional, and spiritual well-being lays the foundation for a life built on resilience and joy.

But no one is an island, and the journey towards healing is often shared. Creating a supportive network emerges as a pivotal strategy. This network isn't merely about surrounding yourself with people but about fostering connections with those who respect, understand, and uplift you. It's about learning to discern genuine support from mere presence, and how to lean on these relationships without losing your newfound autonomy. Within this dynamic interplay of self-reliance and communal support, you'll discover a balanced path forward.

Indeed, the tools and strategies outlined here go beyond mere survival. They are about rewriting the narrative of your life on your own terms, discovering your inherent worth, and stepping into your power. Each page you turn, each practice you embrace, is a step towards not just healing, but thriving—an act of bold defiance against the toxicity that once sought to define your existence. Let this chapter be your guide, your manual for transformation, as you reclaim the life that is rightfully yours.

## Self-Care as Resistance

In the journey towards healing from the invisible wounds inflicted by toxic parenting, self-care emerges not just as an act of personal restoration but as a profound form of resistance. It challenges the narrative that we must remain ensnared in the dysfunctional patterns set by our forebears, offering us a path to reclaim our power and autonomy. This chapter delves into how cultivating a personalized self-care regimen can be a radical act of reclaiming the self that toxic family dynamics sought to undermine.

At its core, self-care in the context of recovering from toxic family environments is about setting boundaries with oneself as much as with others. It's an acknowledgment that you are worthy of care, respect, and love, particularly from yourself. This realization is vital, as many survivors of toxic parenting have internalized the belief that their needs and well-being are secondary, if not altogether irrelevant.

Self-care as resistance begins with the basic premise that you have the right to prioritize your health and happiness. It's a direct counter to the messages of unworthiness or selfishness that toxic parents often impart on their children for attending to their own needs. Engaging in self-care is a declaration that your well-being matters and is essential for a thriving life.

One of the most fundamental aspects of self-care involves physical health. Regular exercise, adequate sleep, and balanced nutrition are not just about maintaining physical well-being but are acts of reclaiming your body from the neglect or abuse it may have experienced. Moreover, these acts strengthen your resilience against stress and emotional turmoil, equipping you better to tackle the challenges that healing from a toxic upbringing presents.

Emotional self-care is equally crucial. For many survivors of toxic parenting, emotional expression was discouraged or punished.

Therefore, allowing yourself to feel, express, and process your emotions is a radical act of taking back your right to emotional existence. Journaling, therapy, and mindfulness practices are powerful tools for emotional self-care that help in decompressing the pent-up feelings and learning healthier emotional regulation.

Mental self-care, often overlooked, involves nurturing your mind through activities that stimulate and engage you intellectually. Whether it's reading, learning a new skill, or engaging in creative pursuits, these activities offer an outlet for the intellect and spirit, providing a sense of accomplishment and purpose outside the narratives imposed by toxic family environments.

Spiritual self-care might not resonate with everyone, but for many, finding a connection to something greater than themselves – whether through organized religion, personal belief systems, or nature – offers a profound source of comfort, strength, and belonging. It's an affirmation that you are part of a larger tapestry of existence, countering the isolation often felt in toxic family situations.

Social self-care is about surrounding yourself with people who affirm your worth and humanity, which toxic upbringing often erodes. Building a chosen family of friends, mentors, and supportive communities can provide the validation and support that was missing. This act of reaching out and forming healthy connections is a powerful form of resistance against the isolating effects of toxic parenting.

Financial self-care is also an essential component, often necessitating a reevaluation of beliefs around money and worth that toxic parents may have instilled. Practicing financial self-care by learning money management skills and making informed decisions about your financial health fosters independence and security, areas often compromised by toxic upbringing.

Practicing self-care also involves recognizing and stepping away from situations or patterns that replicate the toxic dynamics you grew up with. It's about being mindful of the environments and relationships you choose to engage with, ensuring they contribute positively to your healing and well-being. This conscious choice is a form of resistance against the cycle of toxicity.

Self-care requires intentionality and commitment. It's not always easy, especially on difficult days when the shadows of the past loom large. However, it's on these days that self-care is most critical and indeed, most revolutionary. It's a testament to your strength and determination to carve out a healthier path for yourself.

Implementing a self-care regimen tailored to your unique needs and preferences is key. There's no one-size-fits-all approach to self-care; what works wonderfully for one person might not for another. It's essential to explore, experiment, and listen to yourself to discover what forms of self-care are most beneficial for you.

Moreover, self-care is not a static practice but an evolving one. As you grow and your circumstances change, your self-care needs will also shift. Remaining flexible and open to adjusting your self-care practices ensures they continue to serve your best interests.

Lastly, embarking on this journey of self-care as resistance is not a solitary endeavor. While the work is deeply personal, the journey is shared by many. Connecting with others who understand and support your path can provide encouragement, perspective, and strength. It's a reminder that you are not alone in reclaiming your life from the shadows of toxic parenting.

In summary, self-care as resistance is a profound act of defiance against the negative legacy of toxic parenting. It is an assertion of your worth, a commitment to your well-being, and a step towards a life defined not by past hurt but by present healing and future thriving.

Through deliberate, personalized self-care practices, you can not only recover from the effects of a toxic upbringing but flourish, embodying the resilience and strength that have always existed within you.

## Creating a Supportive Network

In the journey of moving beyond the shadows of toxic parenting, one of the most empowering steps you can take is creating a supportive network. This chapter highlights the significance of building connections with those who understand, validate, and uphold your journey towards healing and self-reclamation.

A supportive network isn't just about having people around you; it's about cultivating relationships with individuals who genuinely listen, empathize, and offer support without judgment or reservation. The challenge, however, lies in how to build such a network, especially when past experiences may have eroded your trust in others and in your own judgment of who is safe and who is not.

Initiating this process begins with introspection. Understanding your own needs, boundaries, and what you seek in a supportive relationship is crucial. This may require some soul-searching and self-reflection, aided perhaps by journaling or therapy, to truly get to the root of what you desire in your support system.

Once you have a clearer idea of what you are looking for, the next step is to start small. Look for community groups, whether online or in-person, that resonate with your journey. This could be support groups for survivors of toxic families, workshops on personal growth, or even hobby groups where you can meet people in a neutral setting. The key is to find spaces where you have the potential to connect with others on similar paths or with similar interests.

It's also important to be patient and gentle with yourself during this process. Building a supportive network takes time and may involve some trial and error. You might not instantly find your 'tribe' or feel a deep connection right away, but don't be discouraged. Every interaction is an opportunity to learn more about what you do and don't want in your support network.

Learning to trust again is another crucial aspect. It's understandable to feel hesitant or fearful of opening up after experiencing toxic relationships. However, trusting others—and yourself—is essential for forming genuine connections. This doesn't mean ignoring your instincts or boundaries, but rather, giving yourself permission to test the waters gradually, building trust as you go.

An often overlooked part of creating a supportive network is learning to be a support for others as well. Supportive relationships are reciprocal. By offering your empathy, listening ear, or time to others, you not only contribute to their healing journey but also bolster your own. It's a powerful reminder that you have valuable insights and care to offer, which can further reinforce your self-esteem and healing.

Setting boundaries is also vital in this process. Not every person you meet will be right for your support network, and that's okay. It's important to recognize when a relationship is not contributing positively to your well-being and feel empowered to limit contact or let it go if necessary. Remember, it's about quality, not quantity. A few meaningful, supportive relationships are infinitely more valuable than many superficial ones.

Embrace diversity in your support network as well. Different people can offer various perspectives, experiences, and types of support. Having a wide range of supportive individuals in your life can enrich your journey, providing a more comprehensive system of support that caters to different aspects of your healing and growth.

Don't forget the role of professional support. Therapists, counselors, and coaches can be crucial members of your network, offering guidance, therapeutic support, and tools to navigate the healing process. Their expertise in dealing with the aftermath of toxic relationships can be invaluable in your journey towards healing.

Utilize technology to your advantage. In today's digital age, support can also come in the form of online communities, forums, and social media groups dedicated to healing from toxic parenting. These platforms can offer a sense of belonging and understanding, even when physical meetings aren't possible.

As you build this network, remember to celebrate your progress. Every step you take towards creating a supportive circle is a milestone in your journey of healing. Even when setbacks occur, acknowledging the effort you are putting in to surround yourself with positivity and understanding is crucial.

Lastly, keep your heart open to unexpected sources of support. Sometimes, the most profound connections come from the least expected places or moments. Be open to the possibility that support can present itself in various forms and from different people as you navigate through your journey.

In conclusion, creating a supportive network is a fundamental step in healing from the impact of toxic parenting. It's about intentionally choosing those who bring positivity, understanding, and genuine support into your life. While the journey may have its challenges, the rewards—deep, meaningful connections that empower and uplift you—are immeasurably worth it. Remember, you deserve to be surrounded by a network that not only understands your past but supports your present and celebrates your future.

# Chapter 9:
# Communicating with Toxic Family Members

Communication is a bridge that often seems too frail to cross when it's built over the waters of toxic family connections. Nonetheless, it's a critical aspect of healing and asserting one's autonomy. This chapter delves into the essence of navigating difficult conversations with family members whose behaviors have historically undermined your sense of self and well-being. It's not just about what you say but how you say it and the space you hold for yourself in these interactions. We explore strategies that balance assertiveness with self-preservation, enabling you to express your needs and boundaries without escalating conflict unnecessarily. The choice to engage or to embrace silence comes from a place of empowerment, not defeat. Here, we provide you with tools to recognize when dialogue has the potential to be transformative and when, perhaps, silence carries a more potent message. In communicating with toxic family members, the goal isn't to change them—that may never happen—but to affirm your values and stand in your truth, unshaken by the storms they might conjure. This journey will challenge you to apply empathy and insight in equal measure, fostering healthier dynamics or making peace with the decision to distance, always focusing on what's best for your healing path.

## Navigating Difficult Conversations

Engaging in dialogue with those who have deeply impacted our emotional landscape, especially toxic family members, requires a strategy that balances clarity, empathy, and self-protection. For many, the prospect alone can elicit a wave of anxiety or dread. Yet, learning how to navigate these conversations effectively is a crucial step in healing and potentially shifting the dynamics for the better. It's about finding your voice and using it, not to provoke or win but to express and set boundaries.

Before embarking on these conversations, it's essential to reflect upon what you wish to achieve. Visualize the outcome you desire, but also prepare for the reality that the response you receive might not align with your hopes. This gap often isn't a reflection of the inadequacy in your expression but rather a testament to the deeply ingrained patterns and defenses in toxic family dynamics. Acknowledging this upfront can mitigate disappointment and reinforce your commitment to speaking your truth, regardless of the outcome.

Preparation plays a pivotal role. Draft out the key points you wish to convey. This is not about scripting every word but grounding your thoughts so they don't get lost in the turbulence of emotional exchange. Grounding can serve as an anchor, preventing you from being swept away by the current of reactionary patterns. Think of it as establishing a framework within which you're free to express but not become lost.

It's also vital to choose the right moment. Timing can significantly influence the receptivity of your message. Avoid moments of high stress or conflict, as these can exacerbate defensiveness. Instead, aim for a neutral time when both parties are relatively calm. It demonstrates a thoughtfulness in approach, signaling that your intention is to communicate, not confront.

Throughout the conversation, strive to maintain a stance of assertiveness, which balances honesty with respect for both yourself and the other person. Assertiveness isn't about dominance but about speaking from a place of self-respect and expecting respect in return. This can be a radical departure for those accustomed to dynamics of submission or aggression in toxic relationships.

Active listening plays a crucial role. It's about genuinely trying to understand the perspective of the other person, even if you don't agree. This doesn't mean conceding to their viewpoint but acknowledging their feelings as valid. Such validation can sometimes create a bridge over turbulent emotions, facilitating a more constructive dialogue.

Emotional regulation during these moments cannot be overemphasized. The ability to manage your feelings in real-time allows you to respond rather than react. It's a powerful distinction that can change the course of a conversation. Techniques such as deep breathing, pausing before responding, and maintaining an awareness of physical sensations can help keep your emotions in check.

Navigating triggers is another critical aspect. Recognizing what triggers you and having strategies to manage these in the moment is essential. This might mean taking a brief pause in the conversation, using grounding techniques, or even expressing in the moment, "This is difficult for me to discuss," which can serve as a reminder to both parties of the emotionality involved.

Despite best efforts, some conversations may veer off course. It's important to recognize when dialogue becomes unproductive or harmful. It's okay to take a step back, end the conversation, or suggest revisiting the topic at another time. Protecting your well-being is paramount, and setting a boundary around conversation is a valid and necessary form of self-care.

In instances where progress seems insurmountable, or the conversation reveals a profound impasse, seeking external support can provide another avenue for navigating these relationships. Professional guidance, whether in the form of therapy or mediated conversations, can offer a structured environment where emotions and topics can be explored more safely.

Ultimately, navigating difficult conversations with toxic family members is not about seeking victory but about honoring your truth and protecting your peace. It requires immense courage to face the source of your pain and articulate your needs within spaces that may not have historically honored them. But in doing so, you claim a powerful agency over your healing journey.

Remember, the goal is not to change the other person—that may or may not happen—but to express yourself authentically and set boundaries where needed. This act alone, regardless of the outcome, is a profound step towards healing. You're affirming that your voice matters, drawing a line where old patterns end and new boundaries begin.

It's also worth embracing the concept of compassionate detachment. Understand that you can care about someone without taking on their emotional burdens or letting their behavior dictate your well-being. This isn't easy, particularly with family, where the bonds are deep and complex, but it's crucial for sustaining your health and happiness amid challenging dynamics.

Lastly, celebrate your bravery. Engaging in these conversations is no small feat. It signifies tremendous growth and strength, regardless of the immediate outcomes. Each step taken is a step towards reclaiming your life from the shadows of toxicity and moving forward into light and healing.

As you navigate these waters, remember you're not alone. Many have journeyed this path before you, finding their way through the darkness by holding onto the light of their own truth. Lean on the stories of these survivors, let their courage inspire yours, and step forward with the knowledge that your voice deserves to be heard, and your story deserves its rightful continuation towards healing and peace.

## When to Choose Silence

Transitioning from previous discussions to our current focus requires a delicate shift; stepping from the precipice of confrontation into the silent expanse of internal peace and external neutrality. Silence, too often mistaken for submission, holds unparalleled power in navigating the tumultuous waters of relationships marred by toxicity. This section aims to illuminate those moments when silence becomes not only a tactical decision but a profound act of self-care and boundary-setting.

In the context of dealing with toxic family dynamics, the decision to engage or not can lay the foundation for our emotional well-being. There arises occasional situations where our instinct might push us towards confrontation, hoping therein lies resolution or understanding. Yet, experience teaches that not all words find their mark; sometimes, they ricochet back, intensifying the distress.

Choosing silence is akin to cultivating a garden within where peace can flourish. This does not imply passivity in the face of abuse or neglect but signifies a strategic choice to protect one's emotional energy. In heated moments, when emotions threaten to cloud judgment, silence can serve as a sanctuary, a place to retreat, regroup, and respond from a place of calmness rather than react from a place of hurt.

This decision is exceptionally crucial when engaging with emotionally immature parents. These individuals often lack the capacity to understand or respect boundaries, interpreting attempts at reasonable discourse as challenges or threats. In such instances, silence becomes a powerful boundary. It communicates a refusal to participate in cycles of manipulation or emotional turmoil without having to utter a single word.

Moreover, choosing silence allows for the preservation of self, especially after setting boundaries has been met with resistance or hostility. It can be profoundly liberating to recognize that one's peace does not depend on the approval or understanding of family members entrenched in toxic patterns. Silence in these scenarios isn't giving up; it's stepping up for oneself, affirming that their peace and well-being are paramount.

However, embracing silence requires discernment. Not every situation warrants silence, nor does every interaction with a toxic family member necessitate withdrawal. The key lies in recognizing when silence can be most effective—for instance, when further conversation would only lead to circular arguments, or when any form of engagement is likely to be met with denial or gaslighting.

It's also essential to differentiate between healthy and unhealthy silence. The former is a conscious choice reflecting self-respect and the need for persoanl peace. The latter, however, could be a form of avoidance, a refusal to confront issues that need addressing for one's growth. The balance is delicate and requires constant self-reflection.

In practical terms, choosing silence might mean not responding to provocations, stepping back from conversations that are going nowhere, or literally walking away from situations that threaten your peace. This action—or inaction, rather—serves as a statement of self-worth, a declaration that you value your mental health above engaging in futile debates or defending your choices.

Importantly, silence should also be accompanied by support mechanisms. Isolation is not the goal; connection is. Surrounding oneself with supportive friends, therapists, or communities who understand and affirm your choices is crucial. These support systems provide the strength and affirmation that silence is not a journey undertaken alone but a path chosen to ensure one's personal well-being and growth.

Within this framework, silence also emerges as a profound form of communication. It sends a clear message to toxic family members about your limits and your refusal to be dragged into negative cycles. It communicates to yourself that you are worthy of peace and respect, even if it means distancing yourself from those who should, in an ideal world, be your source of love and support.

Moreover, embracing silence can catalyze personal growth. It offers time for reflection, for asking hard questions about what you truly need and how best to protect your peace. It can be a time of recovery, of healing from past wounds, and preparing for a future where you stand firm in your boundaries and in your understanding of your worth.

In essence, knowing when to choose silence amidst toxic family dynamics is a form of wisdom. It's understanding that not every battle needs to be fought aloud, that sometimes, the most powerful stand you can take is to quietly hold your ground, secure in the knowledge of who you are and the value of your peace.

As we progress through this journey, remember that silence is not an end but a beginning—a foundation upon which you can build a life of resilience, peace, and ultimately, a sense of freedom from the chains of toxicity. It's a path to reclaiming your voice, in your time, on your terms.

In closing, when navigating the complex landscape of toxic familial relationships, it's crucial to remain attuned to your inner compass. There will be times when engagement is necessary and times when withdrawal into silence is the most powerful action. Trusting yourself, honouring your feelings, and prioritizing your peace are the cornerstones of not just surviving but thriving beyond the shadow of toxic influence.

# Chapter 10:
# Building Authentic Relationships After Toxicity

Emerging from the shadows of a toxic upbringing, we find ourselves on the cusp of possibility, yearning for connections that affirm our worth and nurture our souls. The journey towards building authentic relationships after experiencing toxicity is both delicate and profound. It requires a steadfast commitment to cultivating trust and embracing vulnerability, often a daunting endeavor for those who've weathered the storm of manipulative and self-centered family dynamics. As we venture into the realms of healthy relationship dynamics, it's essential to recognize that our past does not dictate our capacity for love and connection. Rather, it serves as a crucible through which our desire for genuineness is refined. This chapter is dedicated to unraveling the intricacies of trust and vulnerability in new relationships, guiding you through the nuanced process of distinguishing between protective self-preservation and the walls that prevent genuine intimacy. Through embracing the lessons of our past, we learn the rhythms of healthy interaction, where communication flourishes, and mutual respect forms the cornerstone of every interaction. As we embark on this path, let us remember that the act of opening our hearts again is not merely a testament to our resilience but a homage to our unyielding spirit of hope and transformation. Building authentic relationships after toxicity is not just about moving beyond our past; it's about stepping into a future replete with possibilities, where connections are rooted in empathy, understanding, and a shared commitment to growth.

## Trust and Vulnerability in New Relationships

Building authentic relationships after enduring a toxic upbringing can feel akin to navigating uncharted waters. The quest for connection, often colored by past hurts and skepticism, requires a leap of faith: to trust again and to be vulnerable with someone new. This venture is not just about moving past fear; it's about cultivating the courage to embrace the possibility of being understood, accepted, and, ultimately, loved.

Trust, a fundamental pillar of any meaningful relationship, can seem like a foreign concept if your formative years were marred by inconsistent affection and broken promises. For those who've grown up under the shadow of emotional manipulation, trust isn't given lightly. It's a treasure, hard-earned and precious, demanding gentle nurturing and patience.

The act of vulnerability, in this context, defies the survival instincts honed during years of self-preservation. Opening up to someone, revealing your thoughts, fears, and deepest emotions, can feel like voluntarily stepping into a minefield. Yet, it is through this very act of vulnerability that genuine connections are forged. By baring our truths, we invite others to do the same, fostering intimacy and understanding.

Begin this journey by acknowledging your own worth. Recognize that your past does not define your capacity to give or receive love. Acknowledge your fears, but don't let them hold you hostage. Instead, let them be your guides, helping you navigate toward relationships that honor and respect your true self.

Set boundaries early on. This might seem counterintuitive when trying to establish closeness, but healthy boundaries are the bedrock of mutual respect and trust. Communicate your needs and limits clearly, and pay attention to how they're received. A partner who respects your boundaries demonstrates their worthiness of your trust.

Trust is built not in grand gestures, but in the daily reliability, the small acts of consistency and care. Look for these signs in potential partners. Do they do what they say they will? Are they present and attentive, or do they dismiss your concerns? These observations can help you gauge whether they're capable of the emotional safety you deserve.

Vulnerability is a gradual process. It's not about laying all your cards on the table at once but rather revealing yourself in layers, at a pace that feels comfortable to you. Acknowledge your bravery in each step you take. Remember, showing your true self is a strength, not a weakness.

Listen to your intuition. Our gut feelings are often the first to sense red flags or green lights in a relationship. If something feels off, it likely is. By the same token, don't ignore the quiet affirmations that you're moving in the right direction. Your instincts are informed by a lifetime of experiences; trust them to guide you now.

Celebrate the milestones, no matter how small they might seem. Each act of trust and moment of vulnerability shared is a victory, a tangible step towards healing. Recognize and honor the progress you're making towards building the healthy, fulfilling relationships you deserve.

It's okay to seek professional help along the way. Therapists and counselors can offer guidance and support as you navigate the complexities of trust and vulnerability. They can offer tools and strategies to help you build self-esteem, set boundaries, and communicate effectively.

Remember, building trust takes time. It's a journey, not a destination. Be patient with yourself and with potential partners.

Healing from a toxic upbringing doesn't happen overnight, but each step forward is a piece of reclaiming your capacity for connection.

Practice self-compassion as you embark on this journey. The path to trust and vulnerability is fraught with potential for self-doubt and criticism. Speak to yourself with the same kindness and understanding you would offer a friend. Recognize that stumbling is part of the process, and it doesn't denote failure.

As you move forward, keep sight of your goals. Envision the kinds of relationships you want to foster. Hold onto the knowledge that you are capable of deep, meaningful connections. Your past has taught you resilience; let your future demonstrate your capacity for love.

Foster connections with others who understand your journey. Support groups, both in-person and online, can offer camaraderie and understanding. Sharing experiences with those who've walked similar paths can enhance feelings of connectedness and provide perspective.

Embrace hope. The journey from the shadows of a toxic upbringing into the light of authentic connection is both challenging and transformative. Trust and vulnerability are acts of courage, signifying not just a desire for something more but a belief in the possibility of achieving it. Hold onto that belief. Let it light your way as you build the fulfilling relationships you not only seek but so richly deserve.

## Learning Healthy Relationship Dynamics

As we navigate through the remnants of a toxic upbringing, understanding and cultivating healthy relationship dynamics becomes a cornerstone of our journey toward healing. This process is not only transformative but essential for those who've grown accustomed to the chaotic, unpredictable, and often painful relational patterns modeled by toxic family members. In this section, we'll delve into the fabric of what constitutes healthy relationships, how to identify them, and most importantly, how to foster them in our own lives.

At the heart of healthy relationship dynamics is the concept of mutual respect. This goes beyond mere tolerance of differences to embody a genuine appreciation for one another's unique qualities and boundaries. Respect is the foundation upon which trust is built, allowing relationships to flourish in an environment of safety and understanding. But how do we cultivate respect in our interactions, especially when our default mechanisms, honed by years of toxic conditioning, skew towards suspicion or defensiveness?

Communication is our most potent tool in rewriting our relational blueprints. Effective communication involves not just the articulation of our thoughts and feelings but active listening. It's about validating the other person's experience, even when we don't fully understand or agree with it. This level of empathy and openness can be challenging to achieve, but it's a skill that, like any other, can be developed over time with practice and patience.

Boundaries are another critical aspect of healthy relationships. They define where we end and where others begin, demarcating what we are comfortable with and what we are not. Setting and respecting boundaries is about honoring ourselves and others, ensuring that our interactions are both affirming and nurturing. Unfortunately, toxic family environments often either disrespect boundaries or teach us to ignore our own, leading to a loss of self-identity and autonomy in relationships.

Eradicating the fear of confrontation is vital in maintaining healthy dynamics. Contrary to what our upbringing may have taught us, confrontation is not synonymous with conflict but can be a pathway to deeper understanding and intimacy. It involves addressing issues head-on with honesty, compassion, and a willingness to find a mutually satisfying resolution. Avoiding or suppressing issues, a common survival tactic in toxic families, only leads to resentment and disconnection.

Trust is the glue that holds the structure of a healthy relationship together. Building trust takes time and consistency, qualities that were likely erratic or absent in a toxic family setting. To foster trust, we must be reliable, keep our promises, and show up as our authentic selves. Trust is equally about believing in the reliability and good intentions of others, challenging the inherent mistrust inculcated by toxic familial interactions.

The journey towards establishing healthy relationship dynamics also involves unlearning the fear of vulnerability. Vulnerability is the courage to be seen and known, with all our imperfections and past hurts. It's the antithesis of the façades we were forced to wear to survive. Embracing vulnerability can be terrifying, yet it's the doorway to genuine connections and the antidote to the loneliness and isolation so common in the aftermath of toxic upbringing.

Equity and equality play significant roles in healthy relationships, ensuring that power and responsibilities are shared fairly. This concept directly contrasts with the power imbalances often present in toxic families, where control and manipulation skew these dynamics. In equitable relationships, decisions are made jointly, with each person's needs, desires, and contributions valued equally.

Moreover, healthy relationships nurture personal growth. They encourage us to evolve, support our dreams, and challenge us to become better versions of ourselves without fear of abandonment. This idea was likely foreign in toxic family settings, where growth was either stunted or rigidly controlled. In a nurturing environment, however, we find the freedom to explore our identities and aspirations.

Recovering from a toxic upbringing involves recognizing and celebrating reciprocity in our relationships. Reciprocity ensures that giving and receiving are balanced, fostering a cycle of generosity and gratitude. Unlike the one-sided transactions characteristic of toxic dynamics, reciprocal relationships are fulfilling and sustainable, negating the fear of being used or overlooked.

Patience is essential as we learn these new ways of connecting with others. Undoing the patterns instilled by years, if not decades, of toxic influence is no small feat. It requires time, reflection, and often the support of therapeutic work or healing communities. This journey back to ourselves and toward healthy relationships is as much about rediscovering who we are as it is about learning how to relate anew.

Support networks play a critical role in this transformation. Seeking out and becoming part of communities that understand and empathize with our experiences can be incredibly validating. These connections can serve as both a mirror reflecting our progress and a safety net catching us when we falter. Whether found in support groups, therapy, online forums, or friendships, these relationships model the dynamics we strive to embody.

Embracing joy and playfulness is an often overlooked but vital element of healthy relationships. Toxic environments can rob us of our capacity to experience joy, making everything seem like an ordeal or a battle. Learning to laugh, enjoying shared activities, and cultivating a sense of wonder about the world can knit bonds deeper and infuse our interactions with lightness and ease.

Lastly, the journey towards healthy relationship dynamics is about nurturing self-compassion. Healing from a toxic upbringing can occasionally make us our own worst critics, replicating the internalized negative voices of our past. Counteracting this through self-compassion not only aids our healing but also enhances our capacity for empathy and understanding in relationships. We learn to extend the kindness, patience, and forgiveness we desperately needed and deserved all along, first to ourselves, then to others.

In essence, stepping into healthy relationship dynamics requires a commitment to self-awareness, growth, and a willingness to challenge old narratives. It's about choosing to break the cycle of toxicity and build anew, not just for our sake but for the sake of all our relationships. This path is not always easy, but it is profoundly rewarding, leading us towards the authentic connections that affirm our worth and nurture our spirits. As we transform our relational landscapes, we reclaim the power to define the trajectory of our lives, proving that the scars of our upbringing, while indelible, do not dictate our future.

# Chapter 11:
# Advocating for Awareness and Change

In the journey of overcoming the shadows cast by a toxic upbringing, advocating for awareness and change not only acts as a beacon of hope for others but also fortifies our own healing path. It's a powerful step towards dismantling the stigma and silence that often shroud family dysfunction, enabling a broader understanding and fostering a supportive community. By raising awareness about toxic family dynamics, we shine a light on a subject that's too often left in the dark, making it clear that those affected are not alone, their struggles are valid, and change is possible. Supporting others on their healing journey, meanwhile, can take many forms—from sharing personal stories and resources to participating in or creating support groups, both online and in real life. This active engagement not only contributes to the collective healing but also emboldens individuals to reclaim their narrative and rewrite their destiny free from past constraints. In doing so, we embrace a movement that not only heals but also transforms, paving the way for a future where understanding, empathy, and support are the norm rather than the exception. The act of advocating isn't just about speaking up; it's about sparking a conversation that leads to a profound societal shift, encouraging individuals to look beyond their circumstances and recognize the strength that lies in community and shared experiences. Together, by fostering awareness and change, we embark on a transformative journey that transcends individual healing and touches the lives of countless others, creating waves of change that ripple through generations.

## Raising Awareness About Toxic Family Dynamics

As we journey deeper into understanding and healing from the effects of toxic family dynamics, it becomes increasingly clear that raising awareness is not just beneficial but essential. Awareness acts as a beacon of hope for those still lost in the fog of confusion and hurt that toxic relationships can create. It's about illuminating paths that were once hidden and offering guidance where there was none.

In exploring toxic family dynamics, we uncover patterns of behavior that perpetuate pain and dysfunction. These patterns are often deeply ingrained, passed down through generations, and can be challenging to recognize from the inside. By raising awareness, we shine a light on these patterns, making them visible to those who are still enmeshed within them and providing an opportunity for change.

The power of sharing stories cannot be underestimated in this context. Stories have the ability to connect us, to make us feel seen and understood. When survivors of toxic family dynamics share their experiences, they not only validate their own feelings but also offer solace to others who feel isolated in their struggles. These narratives contribute significantly to the collective understanding of toxic family dynamics and the multifaceted impact they have on individuals.

Education plays a crucial role in raising awareness. It's about equipping people with the knowledge to identify toxic behaviors and understand their effects on mental and emotional well-being. This education isn't just for survivors; it's also for friends, family members, and professionals who support them. With a deeper understanding of toxic dynamics, we can all become better allies, providing more effective support and advocacy.

Advocacy is another pillar of raising awareness. It involves challenging societal norms that perpetuate the silence and stigma surrounding toxic family relationships. Advocates work to change how these issues are addressed within communities, mental health professions, and legal systems. Through advocacy, we can push for policies and practices that protect and empower survivors.

Utilizing social media as a tool for raising awareness offers both opportunities and challenges. It provides a platform for sharing stories and information widely, reaching people who might not otherwise have access to these resources. However, it also requires careful navigation to ensure that the sharing is done in a way that is supportive and not retraumatizing. The aim is to foster a community of support, understanding, and validation.

Partnerships with educational institutions and healthcare providers can amplify efforts to raise awareness. By integrating information about toxic family dynamics into curricula and training programs, we can ensure that future generations grow up with a better understanding of healthy versus unhealthy relationship dynamics. This includes recognizing the signs of emotional abuse and understanding the importance of setting boundaries.

Creating resources such as books, online courses, and workshops on toxic family dynamics serves as a lasting form of support. These resources not only educate but also offer practical advice and coping strategies for those navigating the path to healing. They can become tools for self-empowerment, helping individuals reclaim their lives from the shadow of toxic influences.

Celebrating progress, no matter how small, is vital in the journey of raising awareness. Every conversation that sparks a moment of realization, every story that touches a heart, and every change in policy that provides better support for survivors is a step forward. These victories, large and small, fuel the collective hope and determination to continue advocating for change.

Engaging in dialogues and discussions about toxic family dynamics in community forums, workshops, and conferences further propels the cause. These platforms allow for the exchange of ideas, fostering a deeper understanding and innovative approaches to healing and supporting survivors. They also help to break down the walls of isolation and shame that many individuals face.

Supporting mental health professionals in recognizing and addressing toxic family dynamics in their practice is crucial. Training and resources can equip them with the skills to better support their clients, providing strategies for healing that acknowledge the complexity of navigating relationships with toxic family members.

The role of self-care in raising awareness cannot be overlooked. For those actively engaged in this work, especially survivors themselves, ensuring personal well-being is essential. It's a reminder that healing is not only about moving past the pain but also about nurturing oneself in the present.

Lastly, building a community of support is perhaps one of the most profound aspects of raising awareness. Knowing that one is not alone, that there is a community of people who understand and share similar experiences, can be incredibly healing. These communities offer a space for validation, compassion, and growth.

As we continue to raise awareness about toxic family dynamics, it's essential to approach this work with empathy, patience, and persistence. The road to change is long and often challenging, but with each step forward, we make progress toward a future where individuals can thrive free from the constraints of toxic relationships. It's about creating a world where respect, understanding, and love define family dynamics, leaving no room for toxicity.

The journey of awareness, education, and advocacy is ongoing. It requires the collective effort of survivors, allies, professionals, and communities coming together with a common goal: to bring about change and healing. Together, we can transform the narrative around toxic family dynamics, offering hope and empowerment to those affected.

## Supporting Others on Their Healing Journey

Helping someone on their path to recovery from the wounds inflicted by toxic parenting is a profoundly compassionate act. It requires patience, understanding, and a deep sense of empathy. For adult children who have lived through such experiences, the journey towards healing is intricate, filled with layers of emotion and periods of both regression and progress.

The initial step in supporting others is recognizing the unique pace at which each person heals. It's critical to acknowledge that healing is not linear. There will be days filled with promise and others where the shadows seem to loom larger than the light. Your role is not to fix them but to stand beside them, offering support and understanding, no matter the stage of their journey.

Listening plays a pivotal role in this process. Sometimes, what a survivor of toxic parenting needs most is a compassionate ear. Listen without judgment or the urge to provide unsolicited advice. The act of listening can be transformative, offering the speaker a sense of validation and understanding they may have long been denied.

Encourage the expression of feelings. Survivors of toxic family dynamics often learn to suppress their emotions as a survival strategy. Encouraging them to express anger, sadness, or frustration in a safe environment can be liberating. It's an integral step in reclaiming their voice and agency.

Empathetic validation is another potent tool. Validating someone's experiences and feelings helps counteract the gaslighting or emotional neglect they might have experienced. It confirms that their feelings are real, valid, and understandable, fostering a sense of emotional safety and trust.

It's also beneficial to gently encourage professional support when appropriate. While your support is invaluable, the expertise of a therapist specializing in toxic family dynamics can offer insights and healing strategies that laypeople cannot. It's a sign of strength, not weakness, to seek such help.

Offer resources and information that might help them understand their experiences better. Sometimes, having access to books, articles, or online communities can provide solace and a sense of not being alone in their struggle. Knowledge can empower and arm individuals with the tools needed for their healing journey.

Respect their boundaries. Survivors of toxic parenting are often working to establish and enforce boundaries, sometimes for the first time. Respecting their limits and preferences is crucial in supporting their journey towards autonomy and self-respect.

Be patient and maintain hope. Healing is a process that takes time and can test the limits of one's patience. Your unwavering support, coupled with a hopeful outlook, can make challenging periods more bearable for those in recovery.

Self-care is equally important for supporters. Supporting someone through such an intense journey can be emotionally taxing. Ensure you're taking care of your mental and emotional well-being to avoid burnout. This might include setting boundaries of your own and seeking support for yourself when needed.

Encourage the building of healthy relationships. As they heal, survivors will benefit from forming connections that are based on mutual respect and understanding. Encourage them to seek out and cultivate relationships that nourish them and reflect their worth.

Understand the role of forgiveness, if it arises. Forgiveness is a personal journey and might not be a goal for everyone. If it does come up, understand that it's a complex process that can't be rushed or imposed. Supporting their stance on forgiveness is part of respecting their healing process.

Highlight the importance of celebrating progress, no matter how small. Acknowledging achievements helps build self-esteem and motivation. Celebrate their courage in facing their past and the steps they're taking to heal.

Finally, empower them to advocate for themselves. Part of the healing journey is learning to stand up for one's needs and desires. Encouraging self-advocacy reinforces their right to a life free from the shadow of toxic upbringing.

Supporting someone on their healing journey is a profoundly meaningful act of love and compassion. It's about offering hope, understanding, and a steadfast presence. Remember, you're not there to lead the way but to walk alongside them, providing support and light during the darker parts of their journey. Through your support, you help them see that healing is possible, and a future defined by their toxic upbringing is not all that there is. Together, you move towards a horizon filled with hope and new possibilities.

# Chapter 12:
# Empowerment: Moving Beyond the Shadow of Toxic Parents

In the journey towards healing, arriving at the doorstep of empowerment marks a profound shift in perspective. This chapter unfolds the transformative process of moving beyond the shackles of toxicity towards a life of self-defined success and happiness. It speaks to the heart and soul of those who've weathered the storm of toxic parenting, guiding them towards the light of personal growth and resilience. We delve into strategies that not only redefine what it means to be successful and happy but also emphasize the cultivation of inner strength that outshines the lingering shadows of the past.

Empowerment is not a mere buzzword here; it is the essence of reclaiming the narrative of one's life. It embodies the courage to redefine personal benchmarks for success, unmarred by the echoes of parental expectations. Happiness, too, takes on a new dimension, steeped in self-acceptance and joy in one's accomplishments, no matter the scale. This chapter encourages you to carve your own path of resilience, reminding you that the power to grow and evolve lies within. Through a blend of insightful strategies, it illuminates the path to a life where past toxicity becomes a backdrop to a future rich in personal fulfillment and growth.

The concepts of resilience and personal growth are interwoven throughout, serving as a beacon for those navigating the aftershocks of toxic influence. It underlines the importance of nurturing an inner sanctuary of strength, which becomes the foundation for thriving against all odds. This chapter is a manifesto for all survivors, asserting that moving beyond the shadow of toxic parents is not only possible but is a journey filled with the promise of rediscovery, empowerment, and untold possibilities for happiness and success on one's own terms.

## Redefining Personal Success and Happiness

In the shadow of toxic upbringing, the concepts of success and happiness often carry burdensome meanings, laden with external expectations and internalized pressures. For many, success was defined by the approval and satisfaction of their parents, regardless of their own desires or well-being. Happiness, if considered at all, was fleeting and conditional, always just out of reach or contingent upon pleasing others. As adults, survivors of toxic families are faced with the daunting task of redefining what these concepts truly mean to them, unshackled from the shadows of the past.

The journey towards redefining personal success and happiness is both liberating and challenging. It invites you to ask profound, sometimes uncomfortable questions: What makes you truly happy? What does success mean beyond material wealth or societal recognition? These questions probe the depths of your soul, asking you to consider what brings you intrinsic joy and fulfillment beyond the superficial or transient.

To embark on this path, it is essential to recognize that your worth is not contingent upon external achievements or the validation of others. You are worthy of love, respect, and happiness simply because you exist. This fundamental shift in perspective lays the groundwork for building a life that reflects your true self, not the expectations imposed by others.

Reclaiming your right to define happiness means understanding that it is okay to prioritize your well-being and desires. Happiness can stem from simple pleasures and moments of connection with yourself and others. It is found in the passion for an activity that resonates with your deepest self, in the quiet moments of contentment, and in the achievement of goals that hold personal significance.

Similarly, redefining success involves distancing yourself from toxic standards of achievement. Success is no longer about climbing a hierarchical ladder at the expense of your mental and emotional well-being but about setting and pursuing goals that align with your values and enhance your sense of fulfillment.

It's vital to embrace the uncertainty that comes with this redefine. The familiar metric of success and happiness handed down by toxic family dynamics may have provided a perverse comfort in its predictability, even as it stifled your growth. Venturing beyond these confines may feel daunting, but it is here, in the uncharted territories of your authentic self, that true happiness and success lie.

Part of redefining these concepts is to cultivate resilience. Toxic upbringing often instills a fear of failure, but viewing failures as stepping stones rather than roadblocks can transform your path forward. Resilience enables you to rebound from setbacks and continue pursuing what genuinely matters to you, imbued with the knowledge that you are learning and growing with every step.

It's also important to nurture self-compassion on this journey. Rewriting the narrative of your life is a process filled with ups and downs. There will be moments of doubt and self-criticism, remnants of the toxic voices from the past. In these moments, self-compassion offers a balm, a gentle reminder that you are doing your best and that you deserve kindness, from yourself most of all.

Establishing a support network plays a crucial role in redefining success and happiness. Surrounding yourself with individuals who respect and support your new definitions can affirm your values and choices. This community becomes a source of strength and encouragement, reflecting back to you the validity of your journey.

It's equally important to set personal boundaries as you embark on this redefine. Boundaries protect your right to personal happiness and success, safeguarding your emotional space from those who may not understand or respect your new path. They serve as a declaration of self-respect and a clear signal of what you will and will not tolerate in your pursuit of a fulfilling life.

Visualization and goal-setting can serve as powerful tools in manifesting your new definitions of success and happiness. Visualizing your ideal life not only clarifies what you truly desire but also acts as a beacon, guiding your choices and actions. Goal-setting, with an emphasis on intrinsic rather than extrinsic rewards, lays out the path to achieving this vision.

Mindfulness and reflection are key practices in this redefine. They encourage presence and awareness, allowing you to savor the moments of happiness and recognize success in its many forms. Through mindfulness, you learn to live fully in the present, appreciating the journey itself, not just the destination.

Lastly, embracing change is fundamental. Redefining success and happiness is an ongoing process, not a one-time event. As you grow and evolve, so too will your definitions of these concepts. Staying open to this evolution ensures that your life remains aligned with your most authentic self, filled with purpose, joy, and fulfillment.

In summary, emerging from the shadow of toxic parenting involves a profound transformation in how you perceive success and happiness. This journey, challenging though it may be, offers the opportunity to live a life true to your deepest desires and values. It's a path towards not just surviving, but thriving, beyond the influence of the past. As you redefine what these concepts mean to you, you reclaim your power and write a new chapter in your story, one where you are the unequivocal author of your happiness and success.

In essence, this redefine is not just about altering perceptions; it's about reclaiming your life. It's about shedding the weight of old narratives and stepping into a space where you can breathe freely, unburdened by others' definitions of worth. Here, in this newfound freedom, lies the potential for boundless joy, fulfillment, and success, crafted on your terms, for your life. The journey may be arduous, yet it promises the invaluable reward of living authentically, passionately, and contentedly.

## Cultivating Resilience and Personal Growth

Moving beyond the shadow of toxic parents isn't an easy journey. It's one that requires courage, persistence, and an incredible amount of resilience. You may have been conditioned to doubt your worth or suppress your true self, but within you is an innate strength waiting to be nurtured and developed. This resilience isn't just about surviving; it's about thriving and creating a life that resonates deeply with your truest self.

Embarking on this path requires a deep understanding that resilience is not an inherent trait but a skill to be cultivated. Every step you take forward, even the minor ones, strengthens your resilience muscle. Start small, celebrating each achievement, knowing that every moment of growth builds upon the last. This incremental progress is crucial; it's the cornerstone of personal development.

One of the first steps in cultivating resilience is recognizing and acknowledging your feelings. All too often, children of toxic parents have been taught to ignore or dismiss their emotions. Give yourself permission to feel everything – the pain, the anger, the sorrow. It's in acknowledging these emotions that healing begins. Mindfulness techniques can be invaluable here, offering a way to observe your feelings without judgement.

The power of positive self-talk in developing resilience cannot be overstated. Your internal dialogue shapes your reality. By consciously shifting negative, self-critical thoughts to ones of self-compassion and support, you transform your internal narrative. This process isn't about denying your experience but rather about affirming your ability to overcome and grow from it.

Building a supportive community plays a pivotal role in nurturing resilience. Surrounding yourself with people who understand and validate your experiences creates a safe space to share your journey. These connections can come from support groups, therapy, or friendships that honor your authentic self. A supportive community not only offers encouragement but also mirrors back the strength and resilience you're building, often at times when you need it most.

Setting boundaries is another critical component. Initially, this may feel uncomfortable, especially if your past has included manipulative or controlling behavior from parents. Nevertheless, healthy boundaries are essential for personal growth. They protect your energy and create the mental and emotional space necessary for healing. Learning to say no, expressing your needs, and distancing yourself from negativity are all acts of self-care that bolster resilience.

Goal setting is also integral to the process of resilience and personal growth. Goals provide direction and a sense of purpose. Start by setting small, achievable objectives focusing on self-improvement and healing. As you accomplish each goal, you'll not only enhance your self-esteem but also reinforce your capability to effect change in your life. Remember, these goals are for you; they should reflect what's truly important and meaningful.

Engaging in regular self-reflection is a powerful tool for resilience. Through reflection, we gain insight into our thoughts, emotions, and behaviors. It allows us to examine our choices, learn from our mistakes, and appreciate our progress. Keeping a journal can be an effective method for self-reflection, offering a private space to process your experiences and celebrate your growth.

Learning new skills and hobbies is another way to cultivate resilience. Dedicating time to activities that bring joy and satisfaction can significantly enhance your sense of self-worth. Whether it's painting, coding, gardening, or anything else, these pursuits offer a constructive outlet for expression and a break from the heaviness of healing.

Physical health plays a vital role in building resilience. Exercise, proper nutrition, and enough sleep do wonders for the body and mind. Physical activity, in particular, is known to reduce symptoms of depression and anxiety. It's not about achieving peak physical fitness but rather about honoring your body's needs and reinforcing the connection between physical wellbeing and mental fortitude.

Finding purpose in your pain might seem like a daunting task, but it can significantly aid in cultivating resilience. Many find that channeling their experiences into action, whether through advocacy, art, or helping others, not only provides healing but also a sense of empowerment. Transforming your suffering into a force for positive change can offer profound personal growth and a deepened connection to others.

Finally, embracing a growth mindset is fundamental. View life as a series of learning opportunities, understanding that setbacks and challenges are not failures but chances to learn and grow. Cultivate curiosity over judgement, and treat yourself with kindness and patience. By adopting a growth mindset, you align yourself with resilience, seeing every experience as a step towards becoming your best self.

Remember, resilience and personal growth are not destinations but journeys. They require time, patience, and persistent effort. There will be setbacks and difficult days, but it's important to recognize these as part of the process. Every challenge you face and overcome reinforces your strength and resilience.

The path of overcoming the influence of toxic parenting is uniquely yours. While the journey is undoubtedly challenging, it's also filled with moments of profound beauty and profound personal growth. Cultivating resilience is about discovering and reclaiming your power, a journey not just of healing but of transformation. As you continue to grow and thrive, remember that you are not defined by your past but by the strength and courage you show in moving beyond it.

Ultimately, cultivating resilience and personal growth is about building a life that feels authentic and fulfilling. It's about breaking free from the constraints of your upbringing and embracing the limitless potential of your true self. You have the strength, the resilience, and the power to create an extraordinary life. Trust in yourself, in your journey, and in the remarkable capacity you have to grow and flourish.

## Online Review Request for This Book

As we close this chapter on empowerment and moving beyond the shadow of toxic parents, it's important to reflect on the journey we've navigated together through this book. Each section was crafted with the intent to offer insights, support, and guidance for those who have experienced the challenges of growing up in a toxic family environment. Now, we reach a moment where your journey can intersect with that of others, through the simple yet impactful act of writing an online review.

# A New Horizon - Life Beyond Toxic Influence

As we've journeyed together through the complexities and challenges of toxic family dynamics, a recurrent theme has emerged: the profound resilience of the human spirit. This final chapter is not just a conclusion but an opening, a gateway to a world where your past does not define you but instead informs a future of possibility, growth, and joy. The path to this new horizon isn't easy or straightforward. It requires courage, persistence, and an unwavering commitment to healing and personal development. Yet, the promise of a life beyond toxic influence is a beacon of hope that makes the journey not just worthwhile, but essential.

The understanding and insights gained from navigating the turbulent waters of toxic upbringing provide a unique perspective on personal growth and happiness. It's an intricate process that involves unpacking years, sometimes decades, of ingrained beliefs and behaviors. The realization that you're not bound by the circumstances of your upbringing can be both liberating and daunting. Liberating, because it opens up a realm of possibilities previously thought unattainable. Daunting, because it places the responsibility of choice squarely on your shoulders.

Setting boundaries with toxic family members is often the first, crucial step toward reclaiming your life. It's an act of self-love that affirms your right to health, happiness, and respect. Boundaries are not walls meant to isolate but protective barriers that ensure your emotional and mental well-being. They allow you to engage in relationships on your terms, based on mutual respect and understanding. The maintenance of these boundaries is an ongoing process, one that may require constant reassessment and adjustment as you grow and evolve.

The healing process is, by nature, deeply personal and varies greatly from individual to individual. It's a journey that might take many forms, from therapy and counseling to self-help and peer support. Embracing this process fully means acknowledging your wounds, understanding their origins, and taking deliberate steps to heal. Healing doesn't imply that the scars of the past will vanish entirely. Rather, it signifies a transition from their controlling influence to a state where they no longer define your existence.

Self-care is an essential component of this journey. It's an act of resistance against the toxic narratives that may have led you to believe that you are unworthy of love, care, and attention. Self-care practices help rebuild the sense of self-worth that toxic upbringing may have eroded. They empower you to create a life that resonates with your true self, not the reflections of others' expectations or demands.

Building authentic relationships after experiencing toxicity is a testament to the human capacity for trust and connection. It involves learning to differentiate between past patterns and present realities, recognizing red flags, and understanding healthy relationship dynamics. Vulnerability, seen in this light, becomes a strength. It's the courage to show up as your true self, knowing that genuine connections are based on honesty and mutual respect.

Reclaiming your life also means redefining personal success and happiness on your terms. It's an opportunity to embrace your passions, pursue your goals, and establish a life that feels meaningful and fulfilling to you. This redefinition is not a negation of your past but an acknowledgment of your power to create a future that reflects your desires, values, and dreams.

The empowerment that comes from moving beyond the shadow of toxic parents is transformative. It's a journey that fosters resilience, cultivates personal growth, and encourages a joyful engagement with life. Empowerment is realizing that while you cannot change the past, you have the power to shape your present and future.

Raising awareness about toxic family dynamics and supporting others on their healing journey extends the circle of healing beyond the individual. It's a contribution to a larger conversation about family, trauma, and recovery. This advocacy not only provides support to those who are still struggling but also promotes a broader understanding and empathy within society.

As we conclude this journey together, it's essential to recognize that the path to a life beyond toxic influence is not linear. It's marked by setbacks and victories, moments of doubt, and periods of profound insight. Each step forward is a testament to your strength, resilience, and unwavering commitment to personal growth.

The new horizon that lies before you is not just a destination but a way of being in the world. It's a life built on authenticity, self-respect, and the understanding that your past does not hold power over your future. As you move forward, remember that healing is not just about leaving something behind but about moving toward something—a life of meaning, connection, and joy.

May your journey beyond toxic influence be filled with discovery, growth, and an ever-deepening sense of peace and fulfillment. The road ahead is yours to shape, guided by the insights and tools you've gained along the way. It's a path that leads not just to recovery but to a profound transformation that touches every aspect of your life.

Embrace this new horizon with an open heart and mind. Let it be a journey of learning, unlearning, and relearning—a journey full of possibilities, guided by the light of your own truth and resilience.

Here's to a future that shines bright with the promise of healing, empowerment, and the freedom to be your truest self.

The horizon ahead is vast and filled with light. Step forward with confidence, knowing that life beyond toxic influence is not just a dream but a reality within your reach. This new chapter is yours to write, each page a testament to your journey from the shadow into the light. Welcome to your new horizon.

# Appendix A:
# Resources for Support and Further Reading

Embarking on a journey toward healing and empowerment can be both exhilarating and daunting. It's a path paved with the potential for profound internal growth, yet it requires courage, commitment, and resources. In this spirit, we've compiled a list of resources to support you on your journey.

## Books and Literature

To further explore the concepts discussed in this book and enhance your understanding of toxic family dynamics, emotional healing, and self-growth, consider delving into additional reading materials. These resources can offer different perspectives, deepen your insights, and provide practical strategies for navigating the complexities of toxic relationships and personal healing.

1. *The Body Keeps the Score: Brain, Mind, and Body in the Healing of Trauma* by Bessel van der Kolk - An invaluable resource that explores the profound impact of trauma on the body and mind, and the pathways towards healing.

2. *Boundaries: When to Say Yes, How to Say No to Take Control of Your Life* by Henry Cloud and John Townsend - A guide to understanding and establishing healthy boundaries in various aspects of life, including family relationships.

3. *Adult Children of Emotionally Immature Parents: How to Heal from Distant, Rejecting, or Self-Involved Parents* by

Lindsay C. Gibson - Offers practical insight into dealing with emotionally immature parents and fostering personal growth and healing.

## Support Groups and Communities

Finding a community of individuals who understand and share similar experiences can be incredibly validating and empowering. Support groups, whether online or in person, can provide a safe space to share your story, listen to others, and learn from each other's journeys.

- Adult Children of Alcoholics/Dysfunctional Families (ACA) - A program for individuals who grew up in alcoholic or dysfunctional families to explore their past and how it affects their current lives.

- CoDA (Codependents Anonymous) - A fellowship of men and women whose common purpose is to develop healthy relationships.

- *Psychology Today* - Offers a comprehensive directory to find support groups focused on issues relating to toxic family dynamics.

## Therapeutic Approaches and Mental Health Professionals

Engaging with a mental health professional can be an integral part of your healing journey. Therapists who specialize in family dynamics, trauma, and personal development can offer personalized guidance and support. Different therapeutic approaches, such as cognitive-behavioral therapy (CBT), dialectical behavior therapy (DBT), and eye movement desensitization and reprocessing (EMDR), can be particularly effective in addressing issues stemming from toxic family relationships.

## Online Resources

The internet is a rich source of information, inspiration, and support. Websites, forums, and social media platforms can connect you with resources, advice, and people from around the world who are on similar paths. Be sure to look for reputable sources and communities that promote healthy discussion and shared growth.

Remember, the path to healing is personal and unique to each individual. What works for one person may not work for another, so be open to exploring different resources to find what resonates with you. Above all, be kind to yourself throughout this process. Healing takes time, and it's okay to move at your own pace and in your own way. You're not alone, and support is available every step of the way.

# Appendix B:
# Self-Care Techniques and Exercises

Embarking on a journey of healing and self-discovery, especially after enduring the turbulence of a toxic upbringing, requires courage, resilience, and a commitment to nurturing oneself. The path to recovery is not linear, it ebbs and flows, offering profound insights, challenges, and opportunities for growth along the way. Within this section, we'll explore a variety of self-care techniques and exercises designed to fortify your mental, emotional, and physical wellbeing. These practices are more than just remedies; they are tools of empowerment, enabling you to reclaim your life and cultivate inner peace and strength.

## Mindfulness and Meditation

Grounding yourself in the present moment can significantly reduce stress, anxiety, and symptoms of depression, common companions for those healing from toxic family dynamics. Begin with just five minutes a day of mindfulness meditation. Sit comfortably, close your eyes if you'd like, and focus solely on your breath. As thoughts come and go, acknowledge them without judgment and return your focus to your breathing. This practice can help anchor you in the now, offering a respite from the turmoil of past memories and future worries.

## Journaling for Emotional Expression and Clarification

Writing can be a powerful tool for understanding and processing your emotions. It provides a safe space to express your innermost thoughts and feelings without fear of judgment or repercussion. Try starting or ending your day with a journaling session, writing about anything that comes to mind, especially your feelings and experiences as you navigate your healing journey. Over time, you may discover patterns, insights, and a deeper understanding of yourself and your needs.

## Physical Wellness: Movement and Nutrition

Caring for your body is just as important as tending to your emotional and mental health. Engaging in any form of physical activity that you enjoy, whether it's walking, yoga, dancing, or weight training, can significantly improve your mood and decrease symptoms of depression and anxiety. Additionally, nurturing your body with balanced nutrition, plenty of water, and restful sleep provides the energy and strength needed to support your healing process.

## Establishing a Self-Care Routine

Create a self-care routine that incorporates elements of mindfulness, physical wellness, and emotional care. This might include setting aside time each day for meditation and journaling, scheduling regular physical activity, and ensuring you're eating nourishing meals and getting enough sleep. Remember, self-care isn't selfish; it's an essential component of your healing journey and a testament to your commitment to reclaiming your life.

## Connection and Support

Isolation can amplify the effects of toxic upbringing, making it crucial to seek connection and support. This may include therapy, support groups, or confiding in trusted friends or family members. Sharing your story and experiences can be incredibly validating and healing. Remember, you're not alone on this journey; there are many who have walked this path before you and many who walk alongside you now.

As you engage with these self-care techniques and exercises, remember to be patient and gentle with yourself. Healing from a toxic upbringing isn't about erasing the past but about understanding, accepting, and growing from it. Each day offers a new opportunity for self-discovery and healing. Embrace this journey with compassion, courage, and an open heart, knowing that you possess the strength and resilience to overcome the challenges posed by your past and create a life filled with peace, joy, and fulfillment.

# Appendix C:
# Tips for Therapists Working with Survivors of
# Toxic Families

Working as a therapist with those who have survived toxic family environments demands a unique blend of sensitivity, insight, and skill. The survivors stepping into your office carry with them stories that may have been untold or misunderstood for years, weighted with complex feelings and challenges. Here are some pivotal tips to guide your therapeutic approach, ensuring it is as effective and compassionate as possible:

## Establishing Trust

Building a foundation of trust is essential. Survivors of toxic families may have deep-rooted trust issues, especially towards authority figures. Emphasize confidentiality, listen without judgment, and affirm their experiences. A secure therapeutic relationship can become a cornerstone of their healing journey.

## Validating Their Feelings

Survivors often come from environments where their feelings were minimized or dismissed. Acknowledge the validity of their emotions, whether it's anger, sadness, guilt, or confusion. Validation can be profoundly healing, helping them understand that their feelings are both real and reasonable.

## Understanding the Dynamics

Familiarize yourself with various toxic family dynamics and the roles family members may play. This understanding can help you recognize patterns in your clients' experiences, making it easier to address specific issues rooted in family dynamics.

## Empowering Your Client

Empowerment is critical. Encourage clients to take control where they can in their lives, recognizing they are not doomed to repeat the toxic patterns they grew up with. Help them discover their strengths and how they can use these to forge a different path.

## Pace the Healing Process

Healing from toxic family trauma is not linear. It's important to pace the therapy according to your client's needs, providing them the space to process their experiences without overwhelming them. Encourage small steps and celebrate progress, no matter how minor it might seem.

## Integrating Self-Care

Teach the importance of self-care. Survivors may have learned to neglect their needs in favor of attending to the needs of their toxic family members. Guide them towards practices that nurture their well-being, emphasize the importance of setting boundaries, and encourage activities that bring them joy and relaxation.

## Focusing on the Whole Person

See beyond the survivor's traumatic experiences. Recognize and foster their interests, talents, and dreams that toxic family dynamics may have overshadowed. Helping them develop a sense of identity separate from their family history can be incredibly liberating.

## Encourage Support Systems

While therapeutic support is invaluable, encouraging clients to build a supportive network outside of therapy can reinforce their healing. Whether it's connecting with friends, support groups, or engaging in community activities, feeling understood and supported by others can significantly impact their recovery.

## Continuous Learning

Lastly, commit to being a lifelong learner about toxic family dynamics and its impact on individuals. The field is ever-evolving, and staying informed about new research, therapeutic techniques, and resources can enhance your practice and the support you provide survivors.

Working with survivors of toxic families is both a challenge and a privilege. As a therapist, you have the opportunity to light a path toward healing and self-discovery for those who have been ensnared in toxic environments. Your empathy, expertise, and dedication can make a profound difference in their lives, guiding them towards a future where they can thrive beyond their past adversities.

## More Books By The Author

In a pursuit to further guide and enlighten those on their path to healing, the author has penned additional resources that delve deeper into understanding personal growth, the dynamics of healing relationships, and empowering strategies for a life filled with self-love and authentic connection.

www.ingramcontent.com/pod-product-compliance
Lightning Source LLC
Chambersburg PA
CBHW031308060726
47590CB00003B/1117